A.

"When we pay close attention to who nonhuman animals really are we can learn valuable lessons from them about friendship, respect, empathy, trust, compassion, and love. However, many cultures tend to devalue other animals, and when differences are noted the animals are usually deemed to be inferior to humans. In this wonderful and most important book, William Crain, a prominent developmental psychologist, who, with his wife Ellen, founded Safe Haven Farm Sanctuary, shares with us stories and data that show many similarities between the emotional lives of rescued farm animals and human children. I came away with a new appreciation of human childhood and I highly recommend this easy to read and inspiring book to a broad audience."

—**Marc Bekoff**, Professor Emeritus, University of Colorado, and co-founder, with Jane Goodall, of Ethologists for the Ethical Treatment of Animals. Author, *Rewilding Our Hearts: Building Pathways of Compassion and Coexistence*

"William Crain reminds us that human beings share deep bonds with nonhuman animals and illustrates how our lives can be enriched through reawakening this connection. How we treat other animals is a reflection of who we are."

—**Gene Baur**, President and cofounder of Farm Sanctuary and author, *Farm Sanctuary: Changing Hearts and Minds about Animals and Food*

"In today's world, it is easy for us to forget how important contact with nature is for children's emotional and spiritual development. This profound and beautiful book reminds us and shows how contact with animals can foster children's compassion and enlarge their humanity."

—**John Robbins**, author, *The Food Revolution* and *Diet for a New America*

"Bill Crain is a leading animal activist. Now he has written a delightful book on his experiences caring for animals. From Mattie the goat to Katie the hen, each story is fascinating and endearing. Readers will empathize with the animals and see why children love them so much."

—**Angi Metler**, Executive Director, Animal Protection League of New Jersey

"Bill Crain takes us on a moving personal journey into the territory of our thought when we were young, a territory which most of us have not since taken the time to explore. He has now cleared a path for broadening our thinking about our place on this planet."

—**Roger Hart**, Professor, The Graduate Center, The City University of New York

"Children can teach us about how to relate with innocence and empathy to the animated world. Magisterial yet modest in tone, Bill Crain's guide is filled with meditations, anecdotes, photographs, and scientific data that manifest our neglected powers to live fully."

—**Elizabeth Goodenough**, editor, *Secret Spaces of Childhood*

"There is much here of importance to those interested in child development, animal behavior, animal rights, and possible spiritual connections between the human, animal, and physical worlds."
—**Jan Drucker**, Professor, Sarah Lawrence College

"The surprise and delight of a child meeting an animal at a farmed animal sanctuary reveals the evolutionary bond of kinship between humans and other animals through the lens of these innocent, but not childish, encounters. That children are enchanted by a chicken or a pig, and the reciprocity that may spring up between them, shows that our interspecies connections go far beyond just keeping a 'pet.' This prospect is vitally explored, with significant implications, by William Crain in this new book."
—**Karen Davis**, President, United Poultry Concerns and author, A Home for Henny, a children's storybook.

"With a powerful combination of tenderness and keen professional insight, William Crain peels back the veneer of social norms to explore how children and animals share a number of fascinating behavioral traits. A series of poignant vignettes shows how the author's personal experiences have changed his own outlook. If you have children or animals in your life, you'll appreciate Crain's superb ability to explain the clinical underpinnings of their complex personalities in a way anyone can easily understand. Now let's hope we can heed his timely wisdom and better protect those entrusted to our stewardship.
—**David Robinson Simon**, author of Meatonomics: How the Rigged Economics of Meat and Dairy Make You Consume Too Much—and How to Eat Better, Live Longer, and Spend Smarter

The Emotional Lives of Animals and Children

....

Insights from a Farm Sanctuary

WILLIAM CRAIN

TURNING
STONE
PRESS

First published in 2014 by
Turning Stone Press, an imprint of
Red Wheel/Weiser, LLC
With offices at:
665 Third Street, Suite 400
San Francisco, CA 94107
www.redwheelweiser.com

ISBN: 978-1-61852-082-1

Cover design by Jim Warner

Cover image: Adam Crain

Printed in the United States of America

10 9 8 7 6 5 4 3 2 1

To my parents, grandchildren,
and Katie, the hen.

Contents

Introduction:
My Decision to Defend Animals

In 2008, my wife Ellen and I founded Safe Haven Farm Sanctuary. It provides a permanent home to animals rescued from slaughter and abusive conditions. We have over seventy animals, including goats, sheep, chickens, turkeys, ducks, partridges, and a mini-horse. This book describes what I have learned about the animals' emotional lives. In addition to my farm work, I am a professor of child psychology, and I also have found that the animals cast light on the emotions of human children. But before I talk about animals and children, I would like to tell you how my efforts to support animals and create a farm sanctuary came about.

It was many years before I took any action on animals' behalf. As a child and teenager, I sometimes worried about the source of the meat I was eating, but these concerns were fleeting.

The occasion that gave me the longest pause occurred when I was fourteen years old. The year was 1958, and I was training for the upcoming high school track season. My teammates and I heard about sensational new track shoes made by Adidas. The shoes were said to be exceptionally light and made of genuine kangaroo leather. We all thought it would be impossible to win without them. I wanted to purchase a pair, but I worried about the kangaroos. I asked a group of teammates, "Do you think they're killing kangaroos just to make these shoes?" They laughed and said they had no idea. My worries lasted a few days, and then I thought to myself, *It couldn't be possible that all the adults in charge could let something so cruel happen.* So I bought a pair of the shoes, concentrated on my running, and for the most part stopped thinking about the kangaroos.

During the next several years, my thoughts about animal welfare remained largely in the background. My focus was on other things—not just track, but my studies and social life. I went to college and graduate school, began a career as a psychology professor, and started a family. I was interested in animals, and I wondered why young children were so interested in them, but these were academic concerns. I still didn't take any action on animals' behalf.

Things began to change one afternoon in the 1970s, when I was thirty-six years old. I was sitting with Ellen and our children in a Burger King restaurant. As I looked at my hamburger, I was suddenly shaken by the thought that I was about to eat an animal. I tried to comfort myself by thinking, *The government wouldn't let people just kill animals for hamburgers whenever people wanted. They probably kill the animals in their old age, after a good life.* I sensed that I was fooling myself, but I pushed the worry out of my mind.

About a year later, I was standing in our suburban backyard, looking at the grass, and decided to become a vegetarian. No specific event or information precipitated my decision. I knew nothing about the awful treatment of animals on factory farms, which supply nearly all the meat Americans eat. The thought just came to me that I would be a more peaceful person if I didn't eat animals. At that moment, an odd sensation came over me: I felt a bit taller.

Eight years later, at the age of forty-five, I added a dimension to my adult life. In addition to my academic work, I began to engage in political activity. I first helped save most of a parcel of woods in my hometown of Teaneck, New Jersey. This was followed by election to the Teaneck school board and civil rights activities.

But despite my increasing political activism, I was slow to act in defense of animals. It wasn't until I was fifty-four years old that I did so. I read a short newspaper article about a proposal to introduce black bear hunts in northern New Jersey, an hour and a half from our home. I thought, *I'd better do something to try to protect the bears*, and I drove upstate to testify at a public hearing.

Why did it take so long for me to act on behalf of animals? One reason was that it took time to separate myself from the mainstream society. Even as a young adult in the Burger King restaurant, I wanted to trust social authority; I wanted to believe the authorities wouldn't tolerate rampant cruelty to animals. I suspect that such trust in authority is widespread, and stems from our species' long childhood. We are dependent on adults for many years, and we need to believe in adult guidance, otherwise we would feel helpless and adrift. It often takes a while to question authority and to form our own judgments. It wasn't until a year after the Burger King experience that I decided to trust my own feelings and stop eating meat.

My decision to testify on behalf of the bears, which came much later, felt more daring. When I became a vegetarian, I knew a few people who were vegetarians, and they seemed to be ordinary folks, so I didn't feel I was entering an entirely new social world. But prior to my decision to testify for the bears, I had never met an animal rights activist—the kind of person whom I imagined to see at the public hearing. I didn't know what they would be like. Would I be joining the ranks of eccentrics or outcasts? It helped enormously that Ellen voiced her support. Ellen simply said, "Do what you think is right. If you want to help the bears, go; there's nothing wrong with that." When I did go to the hearing, I saw that the animal rights activists, like vegetarians, were actually ordinary people.

New Jersey wildlife agencies held several more public hearings on proposed bear hunts. I testified at as many as I could, and was happy that public opposition to the hunts seemed to grow. Many people thought the hunts would be cruel. But the wildlife agencies, whose memberships are dominated by hunters, wanted the hunts. The agencies cited the threats the bears posed. Actually, black bears are shy animals who have never killed a human in New Jersey's recorded history. But new homeowners in rural areas were often afraid of the bears, and hunting advocates kept raising the possibility of a tragedy waiting to happen. Finally, in 2003, New Jersey introduced the first of several six-day hunts. Each year I joined the protest rallies and sometimes engaged in civil disobedience.

In the early 2000s, Ellen, too, was becoming increasingly concerned about animals. Her approach to the issues was more scientific than mine. She did much more reading, gathering factual information on the treatment of animals. I suspect that her objective approach stemmed from her professional life. She was a pediatrician in charge of the emergency department in a large public hospital, where decisions had to be made on the basis of data. She decided, pretty much on the basis of facts alone, that the treatment of animals in modern societies was abysmal.

At this time, we both became concerned about deer hunting in Montauk, a small town on Long Island where our family vacationed. Deer hunting was largely justified as a means of reducing an overabundance of deer. Ellen pointed out that contraception could provide a scientifically sound alternative, and we formed a group to pursue this possibility.

Starting the Sanctuary

Ellen was also reading a good deal about factory farming, and sharing materials with me. She told me how each year in the United States alone, nearly ten billion land animals spend their lives crowded together in huge, windowless sheds, until the day of their slaughter. Most of the animals experience painful illnesses and injuries. Their misery is difficult to even imagine.

Ellen and I frequently discussed what we could do. We donated money to animal welfare organizations, but we wanted to do more. Ellen was interested in farm sanctuaries, which rescue animals that somehow escape factory farms and slaughterhouses—as when a truck derails and the animals run free. Even though the sanctuaries only save a tiny fraction of factory farmed animals, the sanctuaries host visitors and inform them about the conditions of the animals. Could we create one ourselves?

It would be a daunting task. Ellen and I were both busy with our professional lives. But we kept thinking about starting a farm sanctuary, and in 2006 we decided to take the first step. We purchased a broken-down farm with a few acres of pasture in lower Dutchess County, New York. The farm included a barn and two small houses, all in such dilapidated condition that contractors recommended that we tear them down and start over. Then one contractor said he could restore them, and we hired him.

Construction took two years. When it was finished, we named the place Safe Haven Farm Sanctuary and were ready to open it to animals. Because Ellen and I couldn't live permanently at the farm yet, we hired a caretaker, a young woman named Stacy. Stacy, who had been living in Connecticut, drove to the farm with her beautiful mare and a chicken she had named Miss Plucky. The chicken had been abandoned in a pasture with a broken leg. She was our first rescued animal.

A Chance to Learn

I wish I could say my own motive for starting the farm sanctuary was purely altruistic, but I had another goal: I wanted to learn more about animals. I was interested in animals in their own right, and I hoped they also might help me better understand human behavior, especially that of children.

Hearing this last goal, many psychologists will raise their eyebrows. "You cannot generalize from animals to humans" is a long-standing adage in psychology. True, not all psychologists have gone along with this adage. For example, neuroscientists who perform surgical operations on animals' brains hope their findings apply to humans. But such research has largely been motivated by expediency. Researchers have performed operations on animals because it would be difficult or deemed unethical to perform the same operations on human beings. And, in any case, few psychologists would recommend that we look at animals' *natural* behavior, outside the laboratory, for insights into humans.

But there is a striking example of just this approach. It is the work of John Bowlby on children's attachment to caretakers.

Bowlby

Until the 1950s, health professionals were puzzled by the urgency with which toddlers try to maintain proximity to parents. Why do toddlers frequently become so upset when separated from parents? Why, when they are separated for a week or two, do they go through a deep emotional crisis? There was no good theoretical explanation. Many health professionals believed that the children were simply behaving in an immature or neurotic manner. Then Bowlby, who was a psychoanalyst, drew on the observations of a group of biologists called ethologists, who focus on animals' natural behavior.

Bowlby noted that ducklings, lambs, fawns, young chimpanzees, and numerous other young animals also stay close to their mothers. This behavior, most ethologists believe, provides the young ones with protection from predators. If a lamb or infant chimp wandered off alone—or didn't follow the mother in time of danger— the youngster would be quite vulnerable to attack. And throughout most of human beings' evolutionary past, Bowlby suggested, the situation was similar for our children. For millions of years, early humans lived in forests and savannas where they were threatened by predators.

A toddler who didn't stay close to a parent figure was an easy meal for a leopard or a pack of wild dogs.

Bowlby speculated that the child's need to stay close to caretakers might have originated an extremely long time ago—even before humans branched off from other species. This need for proximity probably emerged in our mammalian ancestors and continued to help early humans survive, when predators were still a terrifying presence.

Bowlby cast this need in a new light. When today's toddlers desperately try to maintain contact with parents, they are not behaving neurotically or immaturely. They are driven by a natural, instinctual need. It's a need that is deeply rooted in our species' evolutionary history. Indeed, if human children lacked this need, our species might not even exist today. True, young children don't always cling to parents; children also venture away from them and explore the world. But the need to stay in contact with another person is strong. In fact, Bowlby argued, it is never completely lost, not even among adults.

Bowlby called the need to maintain proximity to caretakers "attachment behavior," and he sparked a vast amount of research. The most influential work was that by his student Mary Ainsworth. Observing infants and mothers in Uganda, Ainsworth tracked the early development of attachment and proposed an attachment pattern that seems very healthy—a pattern in which infants and toddlers balance the need to maintain contact with parents and the need to explore. For example, infants and toddlers often use the mother as a *secure base* from which to investigate the environment. If a mother takes a one- or two-year-old to a new park, the child frequently stays near the mother a few minutes and then ventures some distance away to explore the surroundings. So long as the child feels the mother is available if needed, the child can confidently turn his or her attention to the new and interesting objects.

This secure base behavior is part of a general pattern that Ainsworth called the *secure* pattern, and it describes a majority of children in a wide variety of cultures. And as these children grow up, they generally seem emotionally healthy, coping with life with confidence and energy.

Ainsworth and her colleagues also uncovered two patterns of *insecure attachment*. Some toddlers are so clingy that they have difficulty exploring; other children are so independent that they avoid full relationships with their parents. Children in the insecure patterns more frequently suffer from emotional difficulties as they grow up.

Today, the study of attachment is extremely popular. Psychologists' knowledge of it is quite detailed. But the ethological perspective that started the field has faded into the background. One would hardly know that the initial inspiration came from observations of non-human animals. Moreover, there has been little effort to extend Bowlby's work—to see how the study of animals illuminates other aspects of child development. There have been a few exceptions, but in general there has been a reluctance to follow Bowlby's lead.

Cultural Resistance

I believe this reluctance stems from our cultural values. In Western societies, we draw a sharp line between ourselves and other animals. We speak of the "animal kingdom" as if it were completely separate from us, as if we were not members of it. And we generally consider animals to be very inferior to us. In fact, to call someone an "animal" is usually a derogatory statement.

Psychologists and other scholars are not immune from these cultural attitudes. They share the Western view that our species is special, and they have searched for the capacity that separates us from all the others. "What makes humans unique?"—this has been the great question. Over the years, scholars have proposed various answers, such as the ability to make tools, to use symbols, and to transmit culture. No proposal has held up to scrutiny; each capacity has turned out to be present in some non-human animals, at least to some degree. But the search for human uniqueness continues.

A new field—evolutionary psychology—seems perfect for advancing Bowlby's general approach, examining ways in which other animals might cast light on human behavior. But by and large, this hasn't happened. I suspect the reason is that evolutionary psychologists initially encountered considerable hostility from mainstream psychology. So evolutionary psychologists have shied away from ideas that might offend people, such as the idea that humans are similar to other animals. Instead, evolutionary psychologists have confined their attention to aspects of *human* behavior, such as human mate selection. When they have talked about other animals at all, it has frequently been to say how humans differ from them.

This Book

My book is in the spirit of Bowlby. I talk about animals and draw implications for the lives of human children. True, my effort is somewhat different. Whereas Bowlby drew on vast amounts of published research, I primarily rely on my personal observations. And my effort is more modest. Whereas Bowlby launched a new field in psychology, my main goal is to share observations and offer tentative insights. But, like Bowlby, I do want to call attention to how animal behavior can help us understand our own species.

I have made observations while performing chores or just relaxing with the animals. I have watched them as carefully as I can, and I have written notes after the animals are in bed for the night. I have also kept a small video camera with me and have taken footage whenever I have seen anything new. My approach strikes many of my professional colleagues as very informal, and I agree it is. But I believe it is useful in early phases of research. Moreover, this approach would find sympathy among ethologists, who say that our first task is simply to spend the time to get to know animals. As the pioneering ethologist Konrad Lorenz said, researchers initially need to set aside their presumptions and observe freshly and carefully—"Quite simply, to see what there is."

Ethologists add that we should, ideally, study animals not in confinement but in the wild. We need to see how behavior patterns helped the animals survive in their natural environments. But most of our farm animals do not live in the wild; most spend their daylight hours in fenced pastures and their nights in barns and coops. I wish we could give all our animals a completely free life, allowing them to wander wherever they wish, but I doubt many would survive. If coyotes and foxes didn't get them, human hunters and speeding cars would.

Still, we have tried to give our animals as much freedom as possible. We have extended the pastures for the goats and sheep into a wooded hillside, and we allow our chickens to wander throughout the farm. I will say more on this topic later. And, in any event, I try to follow the ethologists' recommendation to always think about how behavior I see might have developed in the wild.

This book is divided into two parts. Part I discusses six emotional behaviors shared by our animals and human children. Part II returns to the broader social theme of our Western culture's disparagement of animals. I note that children do not initially share the dominant culture's negative view, and that children are taught to detach themselves from animals and devalue them. During my discussion, I emphasize the possibility that animals and children, more commonly than adults, feel at one with nature and her peacefulness—feelings that many people would call spiritual.

~

PART I

Emotions in Animals
and Children

~

⤜ 1 ⤛

Fear

One afternoon I was out in the pasture digging up nettles. After a bit, one of our five goats, Mattie, left the others and came over to me. She put her head next to my hand, and I rubbed her neck. She tilted her head so I could rub it a few seconds more, then she left to rejoin her companions. As she walked away, I had the nice feeling you get when an old friend reaches out to you. I thought about the length of time she had been with us: four and a half years. *That's not a real long time*, I thought, *but we've been through a lot. During her first weeks on the farm she was so scared of humans that I wouldn't have dreamt that she would ever come over to me in such a friendly way.*

I first saw Mattie in a live meat market in the Bronx. Live meat markets allow customers to walk in and select the kind and size of the animal they want slaughtered and butchered. This is done on the premises, so customers can be certain their meat is fresh. In most of the markets, a majority of the animals are chickens, which are usually crammed on top of one another. Many of the markets also sell ducks, guinea hens, rabbits, goats, and sheep.

Ellen and I had driven by this particular market in the Bronx many times, and we had often seen a large sheep standing near the front door. Occasionally we saw one of the goats. Later we learned that most farm sanctuaries oppose the purchase of animals from live meat markets; the purchases, they point out, support the markets' business. We later came to see their point. But at the time, the sight of the animals made us want to do something. So when our farm sanctuary was ready to house animals, in February 2008, we decided to save a few from this market. In particular, I had my mind on the sheep by the door. We also decided we would purchase two goats.

Ellen and I rented a truck, put hay in the back, and drove to the meat market on a chilly Sunday morning. When we arrived, we were joined by our farm's first caretaker, Stacy, and her friend Tom. We walked into the store, talked to the manager, and purchased the sheep we had seen by the door. We also bought a second sheep—a recent arrival who was the only other sheep on the premises. The sheep ran for their lives, but the workers captured them within two or three minutes.

When I turned my attention to the goats, I started feeling upset—even a little sick inside. How could we decide whom to save? Saving two meant determining that the others would die! But the manager didn't ask us to choose. He just told his workers to capture two goats. As soon as the workers stepped into the goats' room, all of them, like the sheep, ran for their lives. The goats were trickier and much more difficult to catch. Although the goats had almost no space to run, it took the workers at least fifteen minutes to grab hold of two of them. So we didn't make any selection; the two goats presented to us were simply the first two the workers could capture.

Once a worker got hold of a sheep or goat, he grabbed the animal by the feet and flung the animal upside down. He then dragged the sheep or goat about thirty feet across the cement floor. When he reached the large scale for weighing, he flung the animal onto it. If the animal was very heavy, another worker helped throw the animal onto the device. We pleaded with the workers to be gentler, but they ignored us. We paid the manager, put makeshift leashes on the animals, and with some pushing from behind, guided them into the back of the truck. They were all trembling and cowering.

On the trip back to the farm, Ellen drove one car, Stacy and Tom drove another car, and I drove the truck with the goats and sheep. The trip would ordinarily take an hour and a half, but I lost contact with the cars and took a wrong turn. For another half hour, I couldn't figure out how to get back on the correct highway. Soon I began to worry about the animals' health. *The truck doors are all closed*, I thought. *If this trip takes longer than I planned, will the animals get enough air?* I knew nothing about such transports. Should I pull the truck over and open its back door to give the animals some air? Or might they jump out and run onto the highway? Finally, I did stop and peek in. They were huddled together and breathing okay.

After three hours of driving, I steered the truck up to the barn. Ellen, Stacy, and Tom were waiting. I sensed that they were irritated by my delay, but they didn't say much because we all had to focus on getting the animals out of the truck and into the barn. All the sheep and goats were scared to death. Pointing to Mattie, Tom said, "This one is trembling something awful!" Tom tried to calm her by stroking her back, but to no avail. He told her, "You're scared now, but you don't know how lucky you are."

Stacy named the animals, and we kept the sheep and goats in a quarantine stall for four weeks, while we had them tested and treated for parasites and other illnesses. During this period, Ellen and I had to work in the city, but we traveled to the farm several days a week. I spent most of my time sitting quietly in a corner of their stall, hoping that if I were unobtrusive, they would get used to me and become less fearful of humans. This seemed to work, but only slightly.

When we finally let the goats and sheep into the pasture, their first act was to inspect the fences. They walked to each section of fence, sniffing and examining it. All the while, the farm's large mare (whom Stacy brought with her when she took the job of caretaker) was watching from outside the fence. Then, when the sheep and goats finished their inspection and drifted to the center of the pasture, the mare began running, jumping, and snorting. To me, she seemed to be saying, "Come on! Play!" The goats and sheep spent about thirty seconds running and jumping, too, but then stopped. They weren't sufficiently comfortable to continue.

Silent Animals, Silent Children

Four days later I heard loud "baa" sounds. At first I didn't know where the sounds came from. Then I saw they were from our own sheep and goats. I suddenly realized that these animals had been silent for over four weeks! And as I thought about the meat market, I didn't remember "baa" sounds there, either. Why were the goats and sheep so silent?

Ethologists such as Konrad Lorenz say that if we wish to understand animal behavior in domestic situations, we need to transpose our images to their natural environments. In the wild, it is highly adaptive for many mammals to be silent in times of danger. Any noise might inform a predator of their whereabouts. For over four weeks, our goats and sheep had gone through a traumatic period when they felt at great risk. So an instinctive response—silence—kicked in.

My thoughts then turned to a human childhood symptom. I had long been puzzled by the fact that young children sometimes stop talking when they lose a parent. For instance, a four-year-old boy who came to my college's mental health clinic became mute for several months after his father left the family and died. The boy didn't exhibit other symptoms; he simply didn't speak. Some of the clinic staff offered a psychoanalytic interpretation. Perhaps, they said, the child unconsciously believed that his words expressed bad thoughts that killed his father. But there was no evidence to support this interpretation. At the farm, it struck me that children who lose parents suddenly feel unprotected, somewhat like our goats and sheep, and this vulnerability triggers an instinctive silence. Children's silence, that is, might be part of our mammalian ancestry, a survival mechanism developed in our evolutionary past.

Other children exhibit "selective mutism." They typically speak at home but not in other situations, such as school. In these cases, too, children might feel unprotected, and the instinctive response of silence, shared with other animals, is activated.

If this speculation has merit, support for it might emerge in children's play therapy. For example, a mute child might hide a child doll when large, "bad" toy figures are near, indicating that the doll feels unprotected. And the therapist's timely acknowledgement of this feeling might help the child feel understood. The child's symptom wouldn't be expected to suddenly disappear, but children do appreciate being understood, which often allows them to become more relaxed and active in the therapy.

Freezing

An evolutionary perspective also might cast light on perplexing behavior in an experimental situation created in the 1960s by Mary Ainsworth. In order to understand toddlers' attachment to their mothers, the mothers are asked to bring their one-year-olds to an unfamiliar room. After a few minutes, the mother briefly leaves her child alone with a research assistant. The mother's departure is distressing to most children. Even children who have developed basic trust in their mother sometimes cry, and they happily greet her when she returns.

This experimental situation has proved to be a very productive research tool. It has enabled researchers to classify children's patterns of attachments to their mothers in consistent and meaningful ways. However, for a long time, some behaviors struck researchers as odd and difficult to classify. The two most common behaviors occur when the mother re-enters the room. In one case, the child approaches the mother, but the child's head is averted. In the second case, the child freezes. The child looks like he or she is in a trance. In 1990, psychologists Mary Main and Judith Solomon concluded that children exhibiting such odd behaviors "lack a strategy" for dealing with the stressful situation, and Main and Solomon created a new attachment category for such behavior, calling it "Disorganized/Disoriented." Studies have found that this general category fits about 14 to 24 percent of toddlers.

Main and her colleagues suspect that the children in this general category are frightened by their mothers. Main's speculation is supported by other research, which suggests that such mothers can fly into unpredictable outbursts of rage. It is understandable, then, that a child in the strange situation might approach her mother for security but also avert her head in case she might be hit.

But why would a child freeze?

When the children freeze, they are not just silent. Their immobile behavior seems more drastic. It strikes many researchers as outright bizarre.

Freezing is more understandable when we consider our evolutionary past. Numerous species of mammals freeze when predators pose an immediate threat. Freezing is adaptive because predators rarely, if ever, attack anything that is perfectly still. It's quite possible that our own distant mammalian ancestors employed this defense, and that it remained adaptive for early humans, after they branched off from other primates. It was an effective defense for the early humans in the forests, open woodlands, and savannas, where leopards and other predators roamed.

My speculation, then, is that the toddlers who freeze are so terribly frightened that an ancient, innate response comes to the fore. If this speculation has merit, the label "disorganized/disoriented" is misleading, as is the conclusion that the toddler "lacks a strategy." Freezing is not just aimless behavior. It's a primordial physiological reaction that evolved because it served a purpose. It enabled our ancestors to survive. It might not seem strategic in modern circumstances, but it was effective for millions of years and is therefore something to which the organism resorts.

By analogy, imagine a group of soldiers who run out of ammunition and must rely on early human weapons— rocks and sticks. The soldiers don't have much chance of victory, but the rocks and sticks do have a purpose. The soldiers' use of them is not merely "disorganized/disoriented" activity. Similarly, in an overwhelmingly frightening situation, some toddlers automatically fall back on one of the organism's early survival mechanisms, freezing.

Therapists and parents might discover that an unexpected benefit accrues when they try to understand seemingly bizarre and disorganized behavior more positively, as an effort to cope and survive. Because children often pick up on adult attitudes, children might feel a new respect, and the overall tone of the adult-child interactions might improve.

≈ 2 ≈

Play

A few weeks after our first goats arrived, we saw a change in one of them, Mattie. She seemed to be gaining weight faster than the others. Our caretaker Stacy was the first to raise the question: "Could she be pregnant?" We asked the veterinarian who made farm calls to see if this was the case, but he couldn't tell. As time went on, Mattie began showing clearer signs of pregnancy and one night she went into labor. Stacy stayed with Mattie through the night. The delivery ran into some difficulty; Stacy had to help position the head. Then the baby, a boy, boomed out. Stacy named him Boomer.

Boomer was full of energy and loved to play. By seven days of age, he was sprinting back and forth in the aisle of the barn, apparently just for the fun of it. When he was ten days old, he ran out to the pasture in the morning and tried to climb up a rock that was about one and a half feet high. But when he reached the top, he slid down backwards, landing with a thud. He climbed back up and jumped down—backwards—and this time he landed perfectly. He climbed up and jumped down several more times. He leapt forwards and backwards, and each time he added a new spin while in the air. He looked like a platform diver experimenting with new stunts. Seeing that I was observing this, Stacy said, "It's funny that he never just jumps, but always tries something new. He's full of antics. He's always playing around."

A few minutes later, I decided to sit on the rock, and Boomer climbed up and rested beside me. But he soon became restless and left in order to run about again. As he sprinted away, he kicked out his legs to the side, first in one direction, then in the other. The side-kicking had a screwball look. Then, as if to show that he had only been fooling around, he leapt high into the air and tucked all four legs under his body in a picture-perfect pose.

Boomer disappeared from my sight into the barn, but then remerged. He walked over to our old rooster, Silky, and stretched his neck out to touch Silky's beak. Silky just stood there. It looked to me like Boomer was saying hello to this elegant old fowl. Then Boomer ran off again, looking for new fun things to do.

All this time, Boomer's mother Mattie looked on from a distance, but she didn't intervene. According to the great Dutch ethologist Niko Tinbergen, this kind of unobtrusive watchfulness is characteristic of the parents in many species. The parents' style, Tinbergen said, is that of "watching all the time, but acting only when the baby demands it."

Play in Children

Like Boomer, human children also like to run, climb, and jump. But human parents rarely stand by as unobtrusively as Mattie did. When we lived on the Upper

West Side in Manhattan, I often watched parents with toddlers on the streets and in the parks. Almost invariably, when a child attempted to climb stairs or jump off a low structure, the adult intervened, saying things such as "Be careful!" and "Hold it. Let me show you." The grown-ups considered their children's actions too risky to leave to the children themselves. And so the young children, who were initially so enthusiastic about climbing and jumping, were deprived of the thrill of independent mastery.

Young human children, of course, don't just run, climb, jump, and engage in physical play. They also engage in symbolic fantasy play, as when they use sticks to represent people and create imaginary scenarios. But modern human adults restrict this make-believe play as well. In an effort to improve academic skills, schools have largely removed free, make-believe play from kindergartens. In addition, many schools have reduced recess and have increased homework in the elementary school grades. As a result, childhood games such as hide-and-seek, snowball fights, jump rope, and informal sports—the games children play on their own, without adult supervision—have become rare. Today's educators consider free play as relatively frivolous—certainly nothing to stand in the way of increased academic instruction.

Is Play Innate?

But watching Boomer made me wonder. Is play so dispensable? Boomer seemed naturally driven to play. His play just seemed to spring up from within. Could play be an innate urge? It appears that all other young mammals play, and from what I have seen, it seems to spontaneously

Mattie and
her newborn,
Boomer.

Young Boomer
and the author.

As an adult,
Boomer
(right) is still
sometimes
playful. Here
he play fights
with a friend.

spring forth in them as well. If you have observed kittens, puppies, colts, fillies, young rabbits, or other young mammals, I bet this has been your impression, too. And young human children also love to play. Could their play express an innate urge that is part of our mammalian heritage? Might it be wired into our genetic plan for healthy development? If so, might adult interference with it have adverse consequences?

For biologists, any consideration of a behavior's innateness raises the question of its survival value. If a behavior became wired into the genes, it must have helped organisms survive. Ethologists have speculated on various possible ways play might confer survival value. A key hypothesis, advanced by Marek Špinka, Ruth Newberry, and Marc Bekoff, is that play develops the capacity to improvise and therefore enables animals to handle unexpected events. If Boomer were to suddenly lose his footing on a hillside rock, or if he needed to jump to escape a predator, he wouldn't panic. In his childhood, he became a specialist in improvisation. He would have a number of acrobatic moves at his disposal, and if need be, he could come up with a new maneuver.

The capacity to improvise also has contributed enormously to our own species' survival. Indeed, our ability to imagine and invent new tools and materials has enabled us to radically transform the environment to meet our needs. We have harnessed the powers of rivers, mined the mountains, and built great cities. True, our creative enterprises have not been uniformly beneficial. Our industrial and technological developments have polluted the air, lakes, and rivers and have destroyed the habitats of countless other species. But this doesn't mean that our capacity to improvise—to create and imagine—should be abandoned. If we are ever to live in greater harmony with nature, we will need to imagine new possibilities.

Such speculations have their place, but if scientists are to consider play to be innate, they will want to see more specific evidence. If the human child's play expresses an innate urge or need, we should see consequences of permitting, rather than frustrating it. Several studies suggest that preschool play enhances cognitive capacities such as problem-solving and creativity, as well as the ability to see things from others' perspectives. In addition, the American Academy of Pediatrics worries that children who are deprived of play become depressed and stressed-out, but more research is needed on this possibility.

In the Emergency Room

I hope researchers will continue to gather evidence on the consequences of our attitudes toward play. In the meantime, I would like to offer two pieces of anecdotal evidence that have made a strong impression on me. The first comes from my wife, Ellen. Reflecting on her experience as an emergency room pediatrician, Ellen tells me that young children play even when they are fairly sick. For example, young children with respitory stress from asthma will nevertheless play with the toys in the waiting room or the equipment in the examining room. The child's playful behavior, she adds, can fool the pediatrician. The pediatrician can easily assume that a child who is playing must be in good health, when this isn't so. It's simply that the impulse to play is so strong that it overrides the child's pain and discomfort.

During the Holocaust

Additional evidence that play is an innate drive comes from George Eisen's little-known account of children in the ghettos and concentration camps of the Holocaust. One might suppose that hunger, anguish, and terror would have completely suppressed their desire to play, but this didn't happen. Summarizing the diaries and reports of victims, Eisen says, "Play burst forth spontaneously and uncontrollably without regard to the external situation." Lacking manufactured toys, the children made their own—out of mud, snow, rags, and bits of wood. When a skeptical interviewer asked a girl how she could have played in Auschwitz, her face lit up and she said, "But I played! I played with nothing! With the snow! With the balls of snow!"

In the Lodz ghetto, children played games with cigarette boxes, which became treasures. One observer wrote, "Children's eyes beg for those boxes, children's hands reach out for them." Hanna Levy-Hass, an inmate of the Bergen-Belsen concentration camp, concluded that children's yearning for play is an "instinctual impulse." "I feel," she wrote, "it is an urge that springs from the soul of the children themselves."

It seems quite possible, then, that the child's urge to play is just as innate in the human child as it is in other young mammals. If so, educational policy makers who ignore it ignore a fundamental and creative aspect of our species.

⇜ 3 ⇝

Freedom

I mentioned how Mattie gave her son Boomer the freedom to play. As Boomer jumped off rocks or darted
about, Mattie kept a watchful eye but never intervened.
The question of freedom is one that Ellen and I think
about a great deal. We wonder about just how much freedom to give the animals.

When I first saw our *adult* goats at play, I actually tried
to stop it. I knew that goats butted heads, but I didn't
know how forcefully they did so. I was startled to see two
of our goats rise upon their hind legs and then hammer
down on each other with their horns. When their horns
hit, the cracking echoed through the hills. I asked Ellen,
"Are they playing or fighting for real? I'm worried they
could hurt each other." She thought they were probably playing, but I was so worried that I stepped between
them. This stopped the headbutting a while, but then
they resumed their battle. After a few more unsuccessful
attempts to stop their butting, I saw that they didn't get
hurt. I began to relax and trust their natural behavior.

(Later I saw that a goat can cause harm by butting
another goat on the side. The side-butt isn't playful. It

occurs when a goat is angry, and it can cause the recipient to fall. I try to prevent this butting, which fortunately is rare. But I had to learn to give our goats the freedom to engage in playful headbutting.)

The issue of freedom goes beyond giving animals a chance to play. The most difficult and persistent question is how far to allow them to roam when predators are about—hawks, foxes, weasels, and coyotes. We have been especially worried about our chickens, partridges, and ducks.

During the first months at the farm, we kept all the chickens in enclosed areas—in barns at night and in large aviaries in the daytime. But after a few months, we began to experiment with allowing the chickens to forage in the open pastures.

Our first major experiment in freedom was with a group of nineteen chickens who had come from Harlem in New York City. A homeless man felt sorry for the chickens awaiting slaughter in a live meat market. Whenever he managed to get together a little money, he purchased one and lifted her over a fence into a vacant lot. People in the neighborhood tossed vegetables into the lot for the chickens to eat, which kept them alive. But some neighbors worried about them and called the ASPCA, who saw that the chickens were malnourished. The chickens had also lacked protection from the elements. So the ASPCA was happy to learn that we would adopt them, and some ASPCA volunteers drove them to our farm.

Ellen and I were distressed to see how much suffering these chickens had gone through. They not only were scrawny and missing many feathers, but were also missing the fronts of their beaks. This was undoubtedly because they had initially been raised on factory farms. The factory farms pack the chickens so tightly together that they fight with their beaks, which means they damage the owners' products. If the owners would just give the chickens a little more room, the fighting would stop. But they can make more money by crowding them together. So they prevent damage by severing the chickens' beaks, usually without anesthesia.

After a few weeks at our farm, the chickens were in good physical condition. But they were irritable. They walked around aimlessly and made rather angry clucking sounds. They became very upset if they saw any human visitors.

One sunny spring morning Ellen and I decided to let them out into the adjoining pasture. I opened the barn door and a few tentatively ventured out. The rest followed. For about an hour, I sat on a rock and watched them forage. They eagerly scratched the ground to see what they could find. They especially loved to dig under leaves. That day they all stayed within a few feet of the barn. Then I steered them back in.

Then came a big surprise. As soon as they were back in the barn, all their irritable sounds disappeared. Instead, the chickens uttered lovely, contented clucking. If you have heard these sounds, you know they possess a maternal and soothing quality. Later that afternoon two visitors came into the barn to see the chickens, and whereas the chickens had previously hated all visitors, the chickens weren't disturbed in the least.

As the weeks progressed, we gave all our chickens increasing amounts of freedom. Today—three years later—the chickens go pretty much where they please as long as we are nearby, except for the road where they could be hit by cars. They are almost always happy. Freedom transformed them.

Chickens foraging.

I would add that I don't think it was just freedom, in and of itself, that made the difference in our chickens' emotions. I have seen so-called "free range chickens" who are free, in the sense that they have room to move, but they couldn't really forage. They could only move on a hard dirt surface. As a result, they didn't seem happy; they didn't emit the sounds of contentment that we have observed. It's not just freedom, then, but the freedom to engage in natural behavior, that leads to deep contentment.

Our most adventurous chickens are a pair who arrived after the Harlem chickens. A woman had purchased them as chicks, but no longer wanted them. They were physically healthy chicks who soon demonstrated their ability to fly over all the fences and travel far from their home barn. One hen is so daring we named her Harriet, after Harriet Tubman, who took great risks to help slaves find freedom through the Underground Railroad. Harriet the hen likes to go off exploring with her friend Bridgette, a strikingly beautiful hen named after Brigitte Bardot, the former actress turned animal rights activist.

Harriet and Bridgette explore most energetically in the evening, when Ellen and I go out to clean the pastures. When they see us head out, they run over to us with great excitement, as if something wonderful is about to happen. Then they forage in the pasture we've entered, pecking and scratching the dirt, grass, and leaves. From all appearances, they seem so engrossed in their foraging that they have forgotten all about us. But when we shift to a new pasture, we always find them there, too.

We're not sure why Harriet and Bridgette are so eager to join us in the pastures. I have told Ellen that I think attachment theory might be relevant. Harriet and Bridgette might enjoy our presence because it gives them a secure base from which to explore. Our presence gives them a sense of security that enables them to investigate their surroundings with great confidence. Ellen disagrees. "I think they want to be around us simply because they're sociable," she tells me. In any event, it's a happy moment when we head out to a pasture and Harriet and Bridgett excitedly run over to be with us.

Still, there is a special, quiet pleasure in watching the Harlem chickens. Sometimes they find loose dirt in which to take a dust bath; sometimes they forage for food; sometimes they just relax in the sun. They suffered enormously for much of their lives, and weren't very happy when they arrived. Now that they are free to move about, they are at peace, and their contentment warms our hearts.

Controlling Childhood

The issue of freedom is at the center of human child-rearing and education. In the United States, adults are controlling children as never before. When toddlers attempt to walk freely out of doors, many adults prevent them from doing so. They strap their toddlers into strollers and push them along. In past generations, older children freely roamed their neighborhoods, but this isn't allowed, either. Parents are too worried about kidnappers and other dangers. Instead, parents fill up much of their children's free time with activities such as music and ballet lessons and enroll their children in organized sports such as Little League and junior soccer. Parents like these activities because they keep their children supervised, and parents also hope the activities will develop their children's talents and put them on the road to prestigious colleges. Parents want the best for their children, but such activities keep their children dependent on adult direction. Children do not play freely, making up their own games and organizing their own time. Even the video games that are so popular today are essentially structured by adult programmers.

These are just some examples of the tightening of adult control, which survey data suggest has intensified since the 1970s. But increasing adult regulation began long before this. If we look back to our species' much earlier days, we see that children once had greater freedom than most of us have ever imagined. This, at least, is what several anthropologists infer from the study of existing hunter-gatherer tribes, which are thought to be the last vestiges of the earliest human groups.

In his recent book, *The World Until Yesterday*, the anthropologist Jared Diamond writes, "At the risk of overgeneralizing, one could say that hunter-gatherers are fiercely egalitarian, and that they don't tell anyone, not even a child, to do anything." Diamond notes, for example, that "among the Martu people of the

Western Australian desert, the worst offense is to impose on a child's will, even if the child is only three years old." Among the Hadza in East Africa and the Pirahã Indians in the Amazon rainforest, toddlers are permitted to wander near fires or to places where knives are present. No adult pulls the child back. Children find out for themselves if something is dangerous.

In his 1933 book, *Land of the Spotted Eagle*, Luther Standing Bear described similar attitudes among his people, the Lakota. He said the Lakota children "grew up without a sense of restriction and confinement." They freely roamed the countryside, taking a keen interest in everything they saw. Of course Lakota children also learned from older children and grownups, but the younger children were never told what to study or what to do. The children simply observed and imitated those whom they admired: "Father never said, 'You must do this,' or 'You must do that.'" When it came to the harshest form of coercion used by whites—physical beatings—the Lakota regarded the practice as "unspeakably low."

If you are interested in reading more about similar attitudes among traditional peoples, I recommend the anthropologist Dorothy Lee's classic book, *Freedom and Culture*. Lee gives many examples of how earlier societies granted children much greater autonomy than we do.

How did our modern, restrictive attitudes come about?

One factor was the increasing size and complexity of societies. Most hunter-gatherer bands were small and very egalitarian, so adults found it more natural to treat children as their equals. As societies became larger, they developed hierarchies of power and status, and children found themselves at the bottom rungs of the ladders.

Even adults who had to take orders from just about everyone could boss their own children around.

Some scholars speculate that another factor was the human control of nature. Hunter-gather societies basically accepted nature as they found her and were grateful for what nature provided. But about ten thousand years ago, as societies were growing in size, they also began to dominate nature. People began domesticating plants and animals. This new kind of domination might have contributed to the idea that it is also acceptable to dominate other people, including children. For example, just as the Europeans who colonized America felt it was proper to "tame" the wilderness, they felt it was acceptable to "tame" the often-impulsive child.

If there was one specific social change that altered adult/child relations, it was the rise of schools. Prior to the 16th century, it was rare for a European child to go to school. The few schools that existed primarily served the clergy. Instead of going to school, most children—even those as young as seven—worked alongside the grown-ups in the crafts and trades of the day. They helped with farm work, performed domestic service, made baskets and blankets, and so on. Many children began their work as apprentices, learning on the job as they observed the more experienced workers.

But in the 16th century the occupational world began to change. With the rise of cities and commerce and the popularity of the printing press, the occupational world began to acquire a white-collar look. New opportunities arose from merchants, bankers, lawyers, and government officials—people who could read and write and do some mathematics. A rising middle class saw bright futures for those who had academic instruction, and middle class parents wanted it for their children. To meet this demand, schools sprouted up in 16th and especially 17th century Europe.

The early schools, however, knew little about teaching, especially teaching young children. For decades, new schools simply replicated those for the clergy, assigning all pupils, even five- and six-year-olds, Latin and Greek texts. The material sailed over the children's heads. The frustrated school masters, assuming that the children weren't working hard enough, resorted to shouting and beatings. They tried to drive the knowledge into the children.

Efforts to control children's learning have persisted ever since. True, teachers eventually had to give up corporal punishment. But education policymakers have tried other ways to force children to learn. A major step was to make education compulsory. Inspired by Prussia, the state of Massachusetts made schooling mandatory in 1855 and the other states followed its lead the next six decades. As a result, an eight-year-old girl or boy, for example, cannot choose to take some time off from school; it's against the law. Education officials have also tried other means of getting children to learn, such as organizing schools like highly disciplined factories. For their part, teachers have tried to motivate children with external rewards and punishments—praise, grades, threats, and criticism.

None of these measures has produced the desired results, and new efforts to exert external control have emerged in recent decades. In recent years, state and municipal governments have tried holding students back in their grades or preventing them from graduating from high school if they perform too low on standardized tests. Few education officials would claim such methods are working, but they continue to recommend them.

From the outset, when schools first started expanding, some people have objected to the pressures they place on children. These critics have generally been outside the educational mainstream, but many have written with eloquence and passion. Their ranks include John Amos Comenius, Jean-Jacques Rousseau, John Dewey, and Maria Montessori.

Montessori, in particular, spoke out against the idea that children need to be pressured to learn. Children, she argued, have an inner need to work on tasks that enable them to perfect their capacities, and if such tasks are available to them, they will freely choose to work on them. It is as if children possess an inner guide that steers them, entirely of their own free will, toward tasks that help them develop their potentials. Adult pressure or supervision becomes unnecessary—even distracting.

Montessori discovered, for example, that young children, given free choice, like tasks in daily living such as cutting vegetables, pouring water, and polishing silver. Montessori speculated that young children like these tasks because they allow the children to perfect emerging motor capacities. Montessori found, in addition, that when children become engrossed in tasks, they often perform them over and over, and when they decide they are finished, they emerge rested and joyful. They seem to have found inner peace. Montessori felt that they were happy and serene because they had been able to develop an emerging capacity.

I have long been impressed by Montessori's observations, and my experiences on our farm have reinforced my sense of their importance. When our Harlem chickens were given the freedom to explore pastures, they became deeply absorbed in foraging and afterward they were happy and serene. Our chickens' contentment was similar to that of the children that Montessori observed. If similar contentment is found in other species as well, it will provide evidence that this response has deep biological roots. Adults will then have even more reason to look for this response as a sign that children are developing naturally.

⪻ 4 ⪼

Care

When our goat Boomer was about two years old, he suddenly didn't seem himself. He grazed with the other goats, but he lacked energy. We called our vet, who examined Boomer at the farm and told us to test Boomer and the other goats for parasites. The results showed that Boomer was suffering from severe anemia from a parasite that was sucking the blood from his stomach. His mother, Mattie, had the same parasite, but her case was not as severe.

The vet said Boomer's life was in imminent danger but the vet didn't have the equipment to save him. He recommended that we drive Boomer to the Tufts veterinary hospital in Massachusetts, which was three hours away. So Ellen and our new caretaker, Karen, put Boomer in the backseat of our Honda Civic. They put Mattie in the car, too. Mattie could have been treated at the farm, but we didn't want Boomer or Mattie to be left alone.

When Boomer reached Tufts, the staff was waiting for him. Once he was out of the car, he tried to walk, but he staggered, so the staff lifted him onto a stretcher. Ellen thought Boomer might lay down, but he stood on the stretcher. Our farm vet later told us that a goat will stand until he or she dies. A sick goat who lies down is a predator's clear target.

In any case, the staff then carried Boomer down a long path to a stall where he would be prepared for surgery. Ellen and Karen watched him go, while Karen held Mattie on a leash. Karen held it tight. She knew that Mattie, like other goats, was rambunctious and loved to explore. On the farm, Mattie had often squeezed through tight fences to see what she could find. And at this hospital, there were many things to attract her—hospital equipment, stacks of hay, and open doors. Mattie could get into considerable trouble.

Then Ellen told Karen: "Let Mattie go free."

Karen was perplexed. It seemed like a crazy idea. But Ellen was the boss, so she followed Ellen's order. Once off the leash, Mattie rushed to catch up with Boomer, and then walked directly behind the stretcher for the rest of the long trip down the hall. For Ellen and Karen, it was a touching sight. Mattie could go wherever she wanted, but all she cared about was her baby.

Boomer and Mattie did recover from the illness. They are very happy animals on our farm, and I have frequently been impressed by their caring behavior toward each other and the other goats. But no animal has impressed me more than a hen named Katie.

Katie, the Hen

Katie was brought to us by a young couple from Brooklyn. They had read that chickens made good pets and had purchased one (whom they named "Katie") at a live meat market. But the landlord wouldn't allow them to keep the hen, so the couple looked for a new home for her, and they found us.

We put Katie in our aviary with a bantam rooster, another hen, and a partridge. The first thing that struck me about Katie was her relationship with the partridge, Cleo.

Cleo came from a hunting club over the hill. The club (the Pawling Mountain Club) charges thousands of dollars to participate in canned hunts. It ships in game birds—pheasants, ducks, and partridges—in boxes, and then releases them for the hunters to shoot. The birds stand little chance. When the birds are released, it's often the first time they have seen the light of day, so they are disoriented and easy to kill. The club likes it this way; it wants its members to go home happy.

But some birds escape, and several have found their way to our farm. We first saw Cleo walking back and forth outside our aviary on a cold winter morning, and we let her in. When we named her, we simply guessed she was a female, which she confirmed a couple weeks later when she laid her first egg. It was a lovely, small egg with a blue tint.

Katie often stood beside Cleo, as if Katie were standing guard over the smaller bird. And Cleo turned to Katie for safety, as I saw one day when I entered the aviary and inadvertently frightened Cleo by walking too directly toward her. Cleo ran over to Katie and huddled next to her, burying her head in Katie's feathers.

One evening I was careless when I opened the aviary's door and Cleo walked out. She darted about, exploring the yard. I happily watched her for a while, but then I couldn't get her back in. I tried to gently coax her from behind, but this didn't work. I next tried standing still while holding the door open, but Cleo was too apprehensive to approach. I said to Ellen, who was working nearby, "I don't see how I'm going to get Cleo to go back in." Ellen said, "I know; I can't think of anything either.

Night is coming, too." Although neither of us said it out loud, were worried about Cleo's exposure to predators; we had seen the remains of a partridge nearby.

Then, while I was holding the door open, Katie walked out of the aviary, stood a moment in front of Cleo, and walked back into the aviary. Cleo then followed Katie back into the aviary.

Scientists warn against reading too much into animals' behavior, but it seemed like Katie acted like a mother guiding her little one back into the home.

Katie and Burdock

It is sometimes claimed that only humans selflessly try to help others. Of course, mothers in other species sometimes sacrifice themselves for their young, but this is explained by the "selfish gene" theory. That is, the mother animal has an instinct to protect her young ones because they carry her own genes. Even if the mother loses her own life, the theory goes, by saving enough progeny she actually increases the number of her own genes.

There are, however, anecdotes about how animals go out of their way to help non-relatives. Animal researcher Robert Sapolsky describes how a baboon named Benjamin rescued a young baboon who was unrelated to him. When the youngster was cornered by a lion, Benjamin ran up to the lion and made threatening gestures until the young one could flee.

Katie's behavior toward Cleo was toward a non-relative, but a clearer example of helping a non-relative occurred with respect to our bantam rooster, Burdock.

One day Ellen and I, as a preventive measure, had to administer medicine to Katie and Burdock. Katie didn't like it when I grabbed her so Ellen could put the medicine in her mouth, but she took it without too much difficulty.

Burdock was another matter. He put up a great fuss. When we tried to catch him, he squawked and flew all about. Every time we thought we could get a hold of him, he darted away. Finally, Burdock flew into a corner, and it appeared that he had run out of escape routes. But as we were about to grab him, Katie ran over and put her body in front of Burdock's, so we couldn't get to him. Ellen and I faced an unexpected obstacle, Katie's body, but we couldn't help admire the way she tried to defend her friend. We finally managed to get around Katie and give Burdock the medicine, although I cannot remember now exactly how we did it. What will always stick in my mind was how Katie tried to intervene on Burdock's behalf.

Katie and Me

I was by now developing the impression that Katie was an unusually caring animal, but I never expected her to show the kind of response she showed to me one day when I was upset by news of a relative's illness. As I went about the farm chores, I felt a bit like crying. Katie walked up to me—which she had never done before—looked at me and stood still in front of me. To many people, it will seem far-fetched to say she was concerned about me. It will sound like I'm anthropomorphizing, attributing human emotions to a non-human animal. But I felt comforted by her. I felt that she saw my pain and cared.

Last Hours

After three years with us, Katie began to weaken. She continued to forage outside the aviary, but she spent more time resting. One morning, she just sat quietly on grass in the aviary. In the afternoon, she sat there with her eyes closed. By this time, the aviary housed three partridges, a chicken hen, and Burdock. In the afternoon all the birds moved near Katie and they remained near her during her last two hours. Burdock stayed closest of all—less than a foot away. On occasion he rose and flapped his wings, but he mostly stood quietly beside her. Then he saw her die. After a few seconds, Burdock rose and flapped his wings with great vigor. Then he crouched down, rose higher than ever, and sent out a piercing rooster's crow.

Children React to Katie on Video

I have made several short videos about our farm, posting them on YouTube and sending the links to friends and colleagues. One video is "Katie, the Hen," which includes the events I have described above. Young children are especially moved by this video. As soon as she had seen the video, one of our grandchildren, five-year-old Caitlin, called to tell me how sorry she was that Katie died. She choked with tears as she said, "I'm sorry . . . I'm sorry . . . about Katie, Grandpa. I'm sorry. But I'm happy her friends were around her."

A parent, Kelly, emailed me that "Our Bess (who is six) watched the video a half dozen times."

Jane, a close friend of our family and long-time nursery school teacher, emailed me about her granddaughter Brooke's response.

Brooke visits us on Wednesday afternoons and today we watched most of your videos. She was particularly moved by "Katie the Hen." She watched it five times. She cried a little each time she watched it, said nothing, and then asked to see it again. Later Brooke called from her home to get it on her computer. I think that she wanted to understand it/death. She asked if she could go to the farm, and I told her that we would take her when she's five (she's almost four now). She asked if you would be there. Thank you for showing us the wonder of these 'common' farm animals.

Jane may be right that her granddaughter watched the video over and over in an attempt to understand death. Young children frequently repeat things in their efforts to master them. Montessori emphasized the way children repeat tasks when they are developing a new cognitive capacity, as when they repeatedly write a letter of the alphabet in the air. During these repetitions, children usually concentrate very deeply, for they urgently wish to develop their abilities.

Focusing on the child's emotional life, the psychoanalyst Bruno Bettelheim observed that children frequently ask to hear a fairy tale or other story over and over. Bettelheim speculated that the child wants to hear the story repeated because it touches on an issue with which he or she is grappling. By hearing it again and again, the child gains the time to think about the issue. For example, a child might want to hear the story of Cinderella many times because the story speaks to the issue of sibling rivalry, which has become the child's major concern. It is not likely, Bettelheim added, that the child is consciously aware of the issue as such. The child is trying to master something on a more unconscious level.

So Jane might be correct that her granddaughter was trying to understand death. This is one reason her granddaughter and other children are attracted to the video and want to see it over and over. At the same time, I believe children's reactions to the Katie video are layered— that children are also affected by other aspects of it. For one thing, children seem moved by Katie's own caring behavior. They are also touched by how the other animals—Burdock, another chicken, Cleo, and the other partridges—stayed next to Katie in her last hours. And, at the most general level, the children's strong reactions to the video reveal how deeply they love and care about animals.

A Caring Volunteer

Children's caring feelings for animals are also quite evident on the farm itself. When young children visit, they almost invariably try to embrace the chickens, turkeys, and other animals, and when they see that the farm has volunteer caretakers, they want to volunteer, too. They want to bring the animals food and water and help out with the cleaning. Some of the children who have asked to volunteer are only five or six years old. Ellen and I cannot supervise children this young and still complete all our chores, but if a parent can take the time to work alongside the child, the child enjoys the activities and being near the animals.

The child who has volunteered the longest is a boy named Jim. Jim began when he was twelve years old, and he is still with us three years later. Jim spontaneously keeps track of every animal on the farm. He periodically counts them, making sure all are accounted for. If he sees that a chicken has wandered too near the road or too deeply into the woods, he runs over and steers the chicken back. To guide the chicken, Ellen showed him how to spread his arms like wings and then walk behind the animal. Jim does this very naturally, and spontaneously walks at the same pace as the chicken.

Recently, a hen went into a hay bin and laid an egg. But she was so deep inside the bin that she had difficulty flying back out. She finally did manage to do so, but afterwards Jim decided to add hay to make her egg-laying spot closer to the opening at the top. Now she jumps out of the bin with ease.

Katie.

Five-year-old child feeds chickens.

Sometimes Jim's younger sister, Miriam, joins him at the farm. Both children have told me that they quarrel a lot at home, but at the farm they work in harmony. Jim's mind is always on the care of the animals, and Miriam, too, is too absorbed in her work to bother arguing with her brother. Because Jim has more farm experience, Miriam readily attends to any task he points out, such as a bucket that needs more water or a gate that needs to be opened.

In school and at home, Jim feels intense academic pressure. His parents want him to excel academically, a desire Jim shares. He becomes anxious when he cannot do exceptionally well. On the farm, he relaxes. His focus turns to the animals. He is in his element.

A Young Teacher Unlocks Children's Compassion

I made a short video, "Children at the Farm," in which Jim is the central character. I like to show the video at conferences on childhood, asking the audience if the video illustrates any childhood qualities that they value. People invariably mention Jim's curiosity, caring, and sense of responsibility. At one conference a young woman, Jacqueline Pilati, talked about the caring attitudes that nature inspired in her class of school children. I was so impressed by her comments that a few days later I asked her to tell me the details of her experience. This is what she told me.

In the 2007–2008 school year, Pilati was a beginning teacher in the South Bronx, a poverty-stricken section of New York City. She was trying to teach twenty-seven children who were dealing with difficult home situations. Many of the children had witnessed domestic abuse or had been abused themselves. Several suffered from fetal alcohol syndrome, and many were diagnosed with attention disorders. The children frequently lived with their grandparents because their parents were incarcerated. In class, Pilati said, the children acted as if they constantly had to defend themselves and their possessions and were quick to violence. They hit each other, flung chairs, and threw objects. "Once a student took off his belt and whipped my co-teacher with it."

A change occurred on Earth Day, when Pilati introduced a recycling lesson that included a film clip of seagulls at a landfill. The children were upset by the sight of the birds eating garbage and living in filth. It was the first time Pilati had seen the children take an interest in anything outside themselves.

Pilati decided to introduce more nature themes. The school officials didn't allow animals in the classroom, but the children began growing lima beans and watching the birds around the school. They built pinecone birdfeeders so the birds could have something healthy to eat. They learned to identify the birds and bonded with one another over their mutual favorites. "Nature," Pilati says, "caused a transformation of something inside. The children became caring and friendly with one another."

Their new, caring attitudes extended to other children outside the school. When Pilati's class heard about the children in the New York Foundling program, Pilati's pupils conducted a fundraising drive to purchase soap, toothbrushes, shampoo, and diapers for the children. Pilati's students needed the items themselves, but they chose to donate them.

Pilati concluded that the way to reach troubled inner city children was through nature activities, and that she had to learn a great deal more about nature to do so. She therefore enrolled in a graduate program in environmental studies, and she currently works as an educational consultant, providing nature activities to school teachers. She believes that nature and animals call forth children's inner urges to protect life.

The Berkeley Schoolyard

Pilati was able to provide her pupils with experiences with birds that helped the children develop their caring feelings. Similar feelings emerged in a landmark project initiated by landscape designer Robin Moore in Berkeley, California. In 1972, Moore and local community members removed a half acre of blacktop at a Berkeley elementary school and replaced it with soil, trees, bushes, and a pond. The nature area was soon inhabited by birds, insects, fish, and small mammals. Most of the animals just appeared at the site. The children, who ranged from kindergarten to the fourth grade, were enthralled. They searched for new animals and watched intently as birds cared for hatchlings. Sometimes the children encountered an injured animal and brought the animal indoors to heal. The children also cared for a few farmed animals.

In 1977, Moore interviewed the graduating fourth graders who had been at the school when the nature area first opened, and their comments revealed strong protective attitudes toward the animals. One recalled, "Kids were trying to throw rocks at the turtle, I got real mad, and me and a friend tried to force them out of the yard." When asked what would happen if the nature area were destroyed, a child said, "We'd go to the school board and tell them they should support nature and be nice to animals." Another said simply, "Nature must be loved."

Do Caring Feelings Emerge Naturally?

Pilati and Moore have suggested that children's caring attitudes emerge quite naturally, without adult instruction. Only a handful of writers have discussed this possibility. One who did was Maria Montessori—and quite a while back! In her 1909 book, *The Montessori Method*, Montessori emphasized children's spontaneous desire to care for animals. She told, for example, how young pupils periodically checked to see if chicks and baby rabbits needed anything, and without any adult telling them to do so. The children, Montessori added, even took a loving interest in earthworms and the movements of larvae in manure, without the aversions that most modern adults have acquired.

Montessori added comments on children's feelings for animals and nature in her 1948 book, *The Discovery of the Child*. She pointed out that although children's positive feelings are instinctive, this does not mean these feelings will develop regardless of the child's environment. Children do need direct experiences with animals and plants for their feelings to grow. By way of analogy, we might think of a little girl with unusual artistic talent. Although her unique talent may be innate, we cannot deprive her of paints and materials and expect her talent to develop. Similarly, we cannot confine a child to an artificial world and expect the child's caring attitudes to thrive and flourish. Tragically, Montessori said, this is precisely the world in which most modern children live. They grow up in synthetic, human-made environments, estranged from nature. So their feelings for nature, which were initially so strong, just wither away. Montessori would have been encouraged by the kinds of experiences provided by Pilati and Moore that bring nature into children's lives.

All the same, Montessori argued that it is only direct experiences with nature—not cultural teaching—that children need. Put children in physical contact with nature and they will spontaneously develop strong feelings for it. But not everyone agrees. Tori Derr, an environmental education consultant who has observed children in New Mexico, argues that physical contact with nature is not enough. Cultural teaching, she says, is critical. Children most readily acquire caring attitudes when adults teach and model these attitudes.

My own view is closer to that of Montessori. From what I have seen, children's caring feelings toward animals grow out of an initial enthusiasm that bursts forth at a very early age—before the adult culture could exert the necessary impact. When Ellen and I lived in Manhattan, I would often sit on the front steps of our apartment building with our dog, a Labrador named Daisy. Almost every time a one-year-old passed by, the child was thrilled by the sight. The children beamed with happiness and squealed with delight as they tried to touch or hug Daisy. Their caretakers usually tried to restrain the children. Similarly, I have frequently noticed that when toddlers, who are just mastering the art of walking, spot a bird, they eagerly try to make contact with the bird and try to follow the bird around. In such instances the child's enthusiasm emerges so early that it seems to be more spontaneous than a product of adult teaching.

In addition, children's protective feelings toward animals are commonly much stronger than those of the adults around them. In a year-long study of four- to six-year-olds in a nursery school, Gene Myers was impressed that,

> Instances of harm to animals were sponta-neously—and urgently—reported by children to parents. . . . When a dead baby bird was brought to class, when a story was told about a puppy being accidentally stepped on, when the baby dove born in the classroom died, when the visiting spider monkeys were confined to a cage: all these provoked concerned or even outraged responses from four- to six-year-olds.

In contrast, the children's teachers and parents generally viewed animals with greater detachment.

Myers doesn't deny that the adult culture exerts a strong effect, but he doesn't think it creates the child's initial love of animals. Indeed, the adult culture's main effect is probably to desensitize the child, as I will discuss in Chapter 9.

A Puzzle

But if children's caring feelings for animals are natural or instinctive, how did they evolve? What was their adaptive value? It would make sense that our ancestors developed caring feelings for other *humans*. Caring feelings for the young, in particular, would have helped human populations survive. But what was the adaptive value of caring for *other species*?

This is a difficult question. But I believe biologist E.O. Wilson and his colleagues have created a theory, which they call the *biophilia hypothesis*, which points in a promising direction.

Biophilia literally means "love of living nature," and Wilson suggests that humans have a genetically influenced interest in other living things. This interest, he says, makes sense when we consider the environment in which our species evolved. For more than 99 percent of human history, our ancestors lived a hunter-gatherer existence in a natural environment—not a mechanical world. A strong interest in animals produced knowledge that helped human populations survive.

Occasionally we catch glimpses of how ancient hunter-gatherers benefited from a detailed knowledge of animal life. A case in point is the tsunami of December, 2004. The tsunami's giant waves crushed the shores of southern India and surrounding lands and islands. The tsunami killed thousands of people. But all the members of the ancient hunter-gatherer tribes on the Nicobar and Andaman islands survived because they knew the animals' warning signs. Before the waves hit, elephants trumpeted and birds took flight, and without hesitation the tribes moved to high ground. In contrast, the modern residents and tourists, unfamiliar with animal behavior, were taken by surprise, and thousands drowned.

In *Land of the Spotted Eagle*, Luther Standing Bear described how knowledge of animals benefited his people, the Lakota, on a day-to-day basis. The calls of the prairie cranes foretold weather changes; the croaking frogs announced the presence of small, hidden springs of water; the snorts of the horses warned of predators. The

Lakota even watched a ground-beetle to learn the location of buffalo herds that human senses could not detect.

Standing Bear's book provides one of the best illustrations of Wilson's proposal that a detailed knowledge of animals aided hunter-gatherers' survival. Standing Bear's book also is valuable for another reason. It indicates how passionately hunter-gatherers could feel about animals. Wilson has sometimes failed to convey this passion. For example, in one article Wilson defined *biophilia* as a "tendency to focus on life and lifelike processes," as if it might be a purely intellectual interest. Standing Bear, in contrast, emphasized how the Lakota felt spiritual bonds with the animals and loved watching them. The Lakota were amazed by animals' alertness, keen senses, and tricks of hiding and disguise—all of which the Lakota tried to emulate. Animals—indeed all of nature—filled Lakota life with wonder and delight. It is my impression, although it needs further study, that similar emotions were widespread among hunter-gatherers around the world.

Standing Bear's account would have brought a smile to the face of psychologist Abraham Maslow. Maslow argued that the fullest understanding of anything—a person, tree, work of art, or animal—emerges from this kind of loving fascination. We see people and objects in all their richness when we love and cherish them.

Once we recognize that an interest in animals can be infused with loving feelings, we can understand how caring attitudes might have developed. If one loves an animal, one wants to aid and protect it. So I am suggesting that because a loving fascination with animals was so highly adaptive for hunter-gatherers, caring feeling naturally emerged as well. They came as part of the same package.

Final Comment

Many philosophers, and many people in general, consider care to be a vital human virtue. But their primary concern is care for other people, not animals. Many people would therefore want to know if children who have a chance to help animals subsequently show a greater interest in helping other humans. In her first grade class, Pilati found that this did occur. After helping birds, the children raised money for children in a foundling home. But Pilati's finding was limited to one group of children. Research on new samples of children is needed. Although I personally believe that caring for animals is important in its own right, I also hope researchers will look into the degree to which caring for animals extends to our fellow humans.

⌇ 5 ⌇

Spirituality

In the Introduction, I wrote a little about my personal story. I mentioned how, at the age of forty-five, I decided I would venture beyond my exclusively academic career; I would also become involved in social issues in my community, Teaneck, New Jersey. This decision eventually led to animal activism, and I would like to tell you what the decision was like.

I felt like I had reached a fork in the road. Teaneck was preparing to destroy a nineteen-acre parcel of woods, the last remaining woodland of any size in our town. There were also other issues calling for attention, including those at the school board. Should I put great efforts into defending the woods and other local causes, even though these efforts would be time consuming? Or should I continue to concentrate on my academic career?

One bleak winter afternoon, I decided to walk through the woods. Perhaps I would see something that would help me decide. But I didn't encounter anything inspiring. Except for a few berries, everything was barren. The woods also had trash in them, and I could hear the traffic the entire time.

Then, as I was leaving, some birds caught my attention, and I lingered a minute outside the woods. I stood and looked at the trees. Suddenly, there was a deep silence just above the treetops. A second later, I felt this same silence in my upper chest. The silence in the sky extended into me. I felt, on a physical level, part of something vast and mysterious.

I didn't know what to make of the experience. I was a mainstream psychologist who valued rational thinking and empirical research—not the realm of the spiritual or mystical. I didn't know anyone with any extensive knowledge about such topics, and I didn't tell anyone about my experience. But I did decide to work very hard to save the woods, and I did soon become involved in Teaneck politics, including running for a seat on the school board.

About ten years later, I came across this poem by Goethe in a book edited by Robert Bly:

Over all the hilltops
Silence,
Among all the treetops
You feel hardly
A breath moving.
The birds fall silent in the woods.
Simply wait! Soon
You too will be silent.

Bly interprets the silence as a metaphor for death, but I think Goethe was referring to a concrete experience similar to mine.

About that time I also decided to write an article on children and nature. I found only a few scattered research studies on the topic, but a few researchers believed that when children spend time in natural settings, they sometimes experience a deep sense of quiet and oneness with nature. These feelings struck me as related to my own and those of Goethe. When I read more about such feelings, I found that scholars considered them to be spiritual.

As I read further, I was surprised that such experiences were not restricted to humans. In fact, they seemed to be more prominent in other-than-human animals. Specifically, other animals also seem drawn to a place just above the treetops or the horizon.

Experiences of Animals

An example is in J. Allen Boone's 1953 book, *Kinship with All Life*, which includes Boone's stories about the dog Strongheart, a large German shepherd who starred in silent films in the 1920s. Boone took care of Strongheart on the West Coast while his owners went to New York to put on a Broadway play.

Boone soon came to believe that Strongheart had inexplicable gifts. For example, Strongheart sometimes seemed to read Boone's mind. But the event that most affected Boone occurred one afternoon when Strongheart led Boone up a high hill. When they reached the top, the dog sat down, faced outward, and stared. Boone was puzzled. Why would Strongheart just want to sit there so quietly when there were so many interesting places all around to explore? Was he watching things down below, fancying himself on guard duty? What was so intensely holding his attention? Then Boone moved closer to Strongheart and discovered that the dog wasn't looking down below at all. His gaze was focused on a point above the horizon line. Whatever he sensed there, it "gave him great satisfaction, great contentment, great peace of mind. That fact was not only written all over him; it was permeating the atmosphere like perfume." Boone added that "I had watched human pilgrims in such meditative poses on sacred mountains in the Orient. I wondered . . . and wondered . . . and wondered . . ."

A similar experience is independently reported by Bill Schul. One evening Schul's German shepherd sat in a reverie, staring at the setting sun. The dog continued to gaze at the horizon after the sun set. Of course the setting sun itself—more than the horizon—might have evoked a special mood in the dog. But in this regard, an observation by Charles Darwin is germane. Darwin noted that although canines are popularly believed to bay at the moon, research reveals that they are actually looking to a fixed point near the horizon.

Similarly, Rachel Carson was once struck by a party of seagulls sitting at the water's edge, staring out over the ocean's horizon. Carson said the gulls were silent and intent. Whatever communion they had at the moment was not with one another, but with whatever they were looking at. When Carson approached them, they didn't startle or fly away, as they ordinarily would have done. They barely took note of her. They simply walked a few feet away and kept staring, completely absorbed.

Finally, a goat at our farm sanctuary will sometimes stand on a rock or hillside and gaze at the horizon in a state of deep peace. It's as if the goat allows the peace of nature to enter into him or her.

These varied anecdotes, then, point to the possibility that there is a point in the lower sky, just above the tree-tops—the horizon—which has special evocative power. It is one of the places in nature which, in the words of

William James, "seem to have a peculiar power of awakening mystical moods."

Peace on the Farm

I occasionally tried to replicate my experience at the Teaneck woods, looking above tree tops and waiting for silence to descend. But it never happened. In the Eastern mystical traditions, individuals undergo intensive training to produce such experiences, but in the West, the experiences seem to just happen to us, as if they have a will of their own.

But I have had better luck at our farm sanctuary. Quite often, when I am cleaning the pastures, and the animals are nearby, a deep sense of peace emerges. The animals are very calm, and their peacefulness seems to extend into the nearby land and it includes me. This sensation isn't restricted to goats looking into the horizon; it often occurs when the goats, sheep, horse, or chickens are just grazing or foraging. Sometimes it comes when I see ducks gliding gracefully on the pond. My feeling is not as powerful as that in the Teaneck woods, but it's definitely out-of-the-ordinary. It is as if the animals bring nature's quiet and peace to me.

What's more, the experience of serenity in the pasture isn't unique to me. One of our farm's caretakers, Mary, independently told me about a similar feeling that comes over her.

Serenity isn't the only emotion that people associate with spirituality. Another is awe. Jane Goodall believes the chimpanzees at the Gombe national park in Tanzania share her feeling of awe at the sight of a waterfall. The chimpanzees swing on branches in a magnificent dance.

Goodall says they are reacting to something they find great and mysterious. But Goodall's observation of chimpanzees at the waterfall hasn't been replicated elsewhere.

Animals in Indigenous Spirituality

I have given a few anecdotes about spiritual experiences that involve animals. Animals also play a major role—indeed, the major role—in the intricate spiritual beliefs of indigenous peoples. This is true, for example, of Lakota vision quests. To prepare for the quests, individuals fast, pray, and purify themselves in a sweat lodge. Then they go off alone into the wilderness to "cry for a vision." They do not always receive a vision, but when they do, it always comes in the form of an animal spirit. The animal becomes the seeker's personal tutor and gives the seeker a message to take back to the tribe.

Animals also are ubiquitous in the cave paintings of the Upper Paleolithic period, painted by hunter-gatherers between about 35,000 and 10,000 years ago. Indeed, the paintings portray little beside animals. Bison, horses, deer, and woolly mammoths are abundant. Human figures are very rare. The paintings are beautiful; the animals appear graceful, almost delicate. In fact, the paintings are so beautiful that scholars have found it difficult to believe that early humans could have created them.

At first, anthropologists conjectured that the drawings served as a form of hunting magic, bringing the animals into contact with the hunters. But there is little correlation between the animals depicted in the drawings and the excavated food remains at the cave sites. A more recent hypothesis is that shamans (spiritual healers) painted them during sacred trances. Their paintings were a way of honoring the animals and sharing their spiritual powers.

However, anthropologists have not really addressed the question of why *animals* are so prevalent—either in vision quests, cave paintings, or hunter-gatherer mythology in general.

As we search for answers, it is important to bear in mind that spirituality includes a feeling of belonging to something much larger than our own species. Native Americans refer to a spiritual presence, the Great Spirit or Great Mystery, that permeates everything—other animals, plants, soil, brooks, rivers, and even stones. Similar ideas are found in Western thought. The English poet William Wordsworth wrote of "a motion and a spirit" that "rolls through all things." Albert Einstein felt that science springs from a kind of religious reverence for the harmony and spirit in the universe that goes far beyond anything the human mind can comprehend.

To many, this mysterious force is a source of balance and peace in the world. Animals would therefore seem especially attuned to this force because they can be so serene. They seem to participate in the deep peace of nature's harmony. This capacity of animals is movingly expressed in a poem by the Kentucky farmer and writer Wendell Berry.

When despair for the world grows in me
and I wake in the night at the least sound
in fear of what my life and my children's lives may be,
I go and lie down where the wood drake
rests in his beauty on the water, and the great heron feeds.
I come into the peace of wild things . . .
I rest in the grace of the world, and am free.

Children

There is evidence that children, too, have a rather special capacity to participate in nature's serenity. Children often seem to let nature's quiet and stillness enter into their senses and bodies.

Perhaps the first researcher to report on such a capacity was Roger Hart. In the early 1970s, Hart decided to write his doctoral dissertation on children's outdoor behavior in a small town in rural Vermont. He spent a year interviewing the town's four- to twelve-year-old children and following them as they engaged in their spontaneous outdoor behavior. Hart noted that although the children were usually active and adventurous, they also liked to sit very quietly beside ponds and brooks, especially sluggish bodies of water inhabited by frogs and insects. Staring into the water, the children entered a kind of meditative state. Hart speculated that the children felt a fluid continuity between themselves and the water. They seemed to feel in themselves the same stillness of the water.

About the same time, in the early 1970s, Robin Moore observed nature's quieting effect at a Berkeley, California, elementary schoolyard. As I briefly mentioned earlier, Moore and members of the school community replaced a half acre of blacktop with soil, vegetation, and a pond, and the nature area was soon inhabited by birds and other small wildlife. When the schoolyard was entirely asphalt, there was constant fighting and bickering. But in the new nature area the children played together more harmoniously, and they were much quieter. This was true of both the boys and the girls, who had previously played apart. In the nature area, they commonly joined together in relaxed conversation. As one child said, "It feels good there. Really quiet. Lots of kids just like to sit around and talk."

Sometimes the children experienced special moments of connection to the natural environment. When the pond is still, Kelli said, "It makes me feel speechless, it's so quiet there. It makes me feel warm inside . . . I just feel nice about myself." Moore called special attention to the girl's empathy with her surroundings. Nature's quiet produced a similar state in her; she felt "speechless." She also felt very good inside, albeit in a way that was difficult to put into words.

In her 1987 autobiography, Sally Morgan, an Australian Aborigine, included a chapter in which her mother, Gladys Corunna, described her own childhood experiences. Corunna was brought up in government homes and was often unhappy. But she found pleasure in watching animals and recalled that as a six-year-old she found a special place.

> I had a crying tree in the bush. It was down near the creek, an old twisted peppermint tree. The limbs curled over to make a seat and its weeping leaves almost covered me completely . . . I'd sit for hours under that peppermint tree, watching the water gurgle over the rocks and listening to the birds. After a while the peace of that place would reach inside me and I wouldn't feel sad any more. When I finally did walk back to the Home, I felt very content.

As environmental psychologist Louise Chawla notes, an especially eloquent description of a childhood sense of oneness with nature is found in the autobiography of Howard Thurman. Thurman was an African American minister whose contributions to the US civil rights

movement are often overlooked. He was primarily respon-
sible for introducing Gandhi's ideas to the movement. In
his autobiography, Thurman described a lonely childhood in Daytona, Florida. He felt comforted by nature
and his special relationships with the woods, night, and
an old oak tree. Each seemed to share its quiet and peace
with him. But his most intense experiences came at the
seashore. A powerful feeling occurred at night when he
felt a deep stillness in the ocean: "I had the sense that all
things, the sand, the sea, the stars, the night, and I were
one lung through which all life breathed. Not only was I
aware of a vast rhythm enveloping all, but I was part of it
and it was part of me."

Such experiences gave Thurman a sense of calm and
the unity of life.

Research by Chawla and by nature educator David
Sobel tentatively suggests that similar experiences occur
in a sizeable minority of children. Sobel believes, moreover, that these experiences are more common in children than in adults.

Sobel bases his speculation on information summa-
rized in two books—one by Edward Robinson, first published in 1977, the other by Edward Hoffman, published
in 1992. Both authors placed queries in newspapers,
inviting readers to send them accounts of experiences
that might be considered spiritual or mystical. A number of respondents said that their most intense nature
experiences occurred in childhood, and that they never
occurred with the same intensity afterwards.

One woman wrote that as a child, "I seemed to have
a more direct relationship with flowers, trees, and animals." She recalled instances in which "there was no barrier" between nature and herself. "As I grew older, I still

Sheep calmly grazing.

Basil, a goat, serenely gazes at horizon.

A ten-year-old girl quietly gazes at the pond.

had a great love of nature and liked to spend holidays in solitary places, particularly the mountains, but this direct contact seemed to fade, and I was sad about it."

The loss of "direct contact" with nature is an important matter. As children grow and become members of our society, they learn to name and categorize what they see, and are not as openly receptive to it. They are no longer totally absorbed in what they encounter, letting their impressions just roll over them and sometimes losing themselves in their experiences. By the time they reach adulthood, they may have detached themselves from nature very thoroughly, viewing nature as little more than human resources and statistical data. I will return to this development in later chapters.

The Turkeys and the Girl Scouts

I have suggested that both animals and children rather commonly experience feelings of peace and oneness with the world. These experiences are generally called "spiritual." Based on my observations of animals' serenity at the farm, my guess is that these experiences are even more common in animals than in children, but the entire topic needs much fuller study.

However, many people will find it difficult to believe that animals share anything similar to human spirituality. Francis Collins, who has headed the Human Genome Project and also has written about his religious views, says that spirituality is confined to our species alone. Others have voiced the same opinion. On this issue, I would like to summarize an event at our farm sanctuary.

One day a troop of Girl Scouts visited our farm. The girls—nine in all—presented us with gifts for the farm and then held a ceremony in the barn. They gathered in a circle and stood quietly while the girls took turns reading pledges to respect all animals. They vowed to cherish always the love and beauty animals bestow upon us. They pledged to protect all animals' right to a natural death and "to console them and ask that the angels gather them in their arms." The statements were very solemn and moving.

What happened next was something none of us who worked at the farm would have ever expected. Soon after the Scouts began reading their pledges, our four turkeys, who until that point had spent every waking moment noisily milling about, joined the circle. Each turkey moved to a separate part of the circle. Each sat in perfect stillness, with her eyes on the reader. It was as if the turkeys were listening to the pledges and were as moved as the rest of us. All the humans present were astonished.

I suspect there was a spiritual element—an attitude of quiet reverence—in the Scouts' ceremony that the turkeys responded to. The turkeys could not have understood the Scouts' words, but they felt the Scouts' inward quietness.

⇜ 6 ⇝

Resilience

When the real estate agent initially showed us our farm, we heard gunshots in the background. "Yes, there is hunting nearby," she told us. "I don't like to hear it. But it's the only drawback." Indeed, the farm has beautiful scenery, including woods and a large pond.

The gunfire turned out to be quite frequent. It comes from a hunting club over the hill, about a mile away. I mentioned the club in Chapter 4. Here I will describe it in a bit more detail. I will also describe how we have tried to help the ducks who have escaped from it. During our efforts, we have learned about their modes of resilience, their ways of coping with adversity.

We Visit the Hunting Club

The first people we asked about the club didn't know much about it. So after the farm's construction was complete, Ellen and I drove over to take a look. Signs at the entrance read, "No Trespassing" and "Members Only."

Ellen, who was driving the car, said, "Let's get a closer look anyway. We'll say we're interested in joining."

As we drove toward the buildings we heard the howls of the dogs in the kennels. We came to a narrow building where there were at least twenty large dog food bags filled with dead pheasants. Ellen quickly took a photo from the car window. Then a man strode over and ordered us to get out immediately. He didn't wait for Ellen's explanation about wishing to join the club.

Ellen was set on getting additional photos, so we drove back to the club a week later. This time we saw stacks of boxes labeled "game birds" and dead birds on a back table. A short distance away, two dead deer hung upside down on a line, in preparation for butchering. Ellen snapped a couple additional photos. Then another club official demanded that we leave.

Over the next few months, I learned more about the hunting club. For a substantial membership fee, the club offers skeet shooting (shooting at clay targets) as well as hunting on its enclosed land. The "game bird" boxes that we saw contain mallard ducks, pheasants, or partridges, which are shipped to the club from factory farms. The club releases about fifteen birds each time a member comes for a hunt. Because the birds were raised in indoor factory farms, each bird's release is probably the first time the animal has seen the light of day. The bird hasn't had time to orient to the surroundings and is an easy target. Miraculously, birds occasionally escape, and some come to our farm and the surrounding area. Mallard ducks are the most common. The escapees are the lucky ones, but their lives are still at great risk.

Dead birds on back table at hunting club.

Facing Long Odds

Neighbors told us that every fall they had seen several mallard ducks on our pond, but when the pond froze during the winter, the ducks were gone. The neighbors thought predators got them. When ducks have access to water, they have a good chance of avoiding predators such as foxes and coyotes. Ducks can easily out-swim them. But when our pond froze over, they had no water to escape to.

During our second winter on the farm, one neighbor, Dan, phoned to tell me that twelve ducks had been near his house. He said they had sought protection from a snowstorm. "But only one is left," Dan said. "The others wandered off and I think they froze or starved to death. I've seen a few frozen in the snow."

Dan asked if we would take the remaining duck, a male mallard, and Ellen and I agreed to adopt him. We expanded an aviary and installed a small pond in which he could swim. We also adopted another duck, unwanted by his owner, so our first duck would have a friend.

But much larger action was needed. Clearly, the best way to save the birds would be to stop the club from shooting them. I made phone calls to people who were known as animal lovers to see what they thought about circulating a petition. Everyone said any effort to stop the hunting was futile. The club is too entrenched in the town, they said, adding that it makes large financial donations to town organizations. I went to a town board meeting and spoke about the cruelty to the animals. But the board members just listened politely. When I finished speaking, the chairperson said, "Thank you," and the board turned to other business. Stopping this hunting would be slow and difficult.

For the short run, Ellen and I tried to think of ways to help the birds who found their way to us. Because ducks were by far the most numerous, they were our main focus. In the fall after we adopted the two ducks, we installed two bubblers, small machines that stirred up water in the pond. We hoped they would prevent an area of the pond from freezing.

We watched closely as ducks came to our pond that fall. Some came on their own, but we frequently spotted a duck wandering aimlessly in the woods and steered the duck toward the water. We walked behind the bird, who waddled forward to avoid us. As soon as the duck saw the others on the pond, he or she became excited and hurried down to the water. We worried that the newcomers might not be welcomed, but they always were.

The Ducks Organize

In November, when there were about fifteen ducks on the pond, I began to give them some corn and grain in the mornings. The first time I put the food on the shore, they ate it eagerly. But one duck stayed in the water. He was a male who appeared to be weak. Periodically, he flapped a wing, as if injured. I thought, *Oh, no. He's sick or injured. But he's far from the shore. How could I ever get him to take him to a vet?*

That day, I walked down from the barns to the pond several times to get a better look at him. Surprisingly, he was large and appeared to be strong. He had exceptionally bright coloring. When I put out more food the next morning, he again stayed back. But this time, after the ducks had eaten for a few minutes, he swam to the shore, looked at the others, perhaps made some sound, and then swam back toward the center of the pond. And when he swam away, the others followed. He was the leader!

Over the next few days, this behavior sequence occurred at every feeding. While the others ate on shore, he stayed back. He was apparently standing guard until he decided it was time to lead them back to the safety of the water. His behavior resembled that of our roosters, who watch patiently while the hens eat or forage, and then decide when it's time to stop and return to shelter. As I thought back to the first time I fed the ducks, when he appeared injured, it occurred to me that he was engaging in a diversionary tactic, as birds sometimes do when predators are near.

This duck's leadership marked the beginning of a social organization. From that time on, I was repeatedly impressed by the extent to which they behaved as a group. Sometimes, for example, ducks swam in a circle, as if patrolling an area. Once I saw a duck fly in from afar, look at all the ducks like a football quarterback talking to a huddle, and then swim away—with all the others following. I didn't know what the behavior meant, but it was definitely organized.

That fall, two geese came to the pond. They were much larger than the ducks, and they soon began to dominate the feedings. When ducks came near the corn and grain, the geese chased them away. Then, a few days later, something surprising happened. Several ducks huddled in the middle of the pond and then flew, *en masse*, toward the geese. They swam toward the geese with their heads low, in attack mode. The startled geese flew away. When they returned, a truce developed, and the ducks and geese shared the food.

Later I was re-reading Konrad Lorenz's book, *On Aggression*, and learned that it is not uncommon for prey to join together in groups and attack even the most fearsome predators. It is called "mobbing." You might have seen birds flock together and harass a cat. We recently saw a similar example among our sheep. One afternoon our dog Daisy, a Labrador Retriever, followed us into a pasture and began barking. The sheep were initially frightened. Then they huddled up and ran at her as one. Our Lab scurried away.

Winter and Spring

In late October and early November, I often stood above the pond and watched the ducks for long stretches of time. They swam so gracefully. Sometimes they dove upside down for plants, or flew about and made smooth landings. Much of their behavior seemed to be just for the fun of it.

But soon came winter, with its cold winds and snow storms. The pond froze, but a small section did not. The bubblers worked! The ducks spent most of their time swimming in the water, or sitting on the ice at the water's edge. On especially cold days, they huddled together on the ice. The winter was harsh, but all the ducks but one—twenty-three out of the twenty-four—lived through it. (We do not know what happened to the one who went missing.)

In the spring, the ducks' organized behavior temporarily came apart. They engaged in a great deal of posturing and fighting. The males chased one another away as they pursued the females, and the females frequently ran or flew to escape unwanted overtures. It was every duck for himself or herself.

Then the females began spending time in the brush, building nests. The males stopped fighting. Their behavior became organized once again. They resumed swimming together. Unfortunately, the females didn't succeed in producing ducklings that spring. We saw eggs in highly visible places, such as the open grass. Several eggs were eaten, with only shells remaining on the ground. The females didn't seem to quite know what they were doing.

This year's events have been generally similar, but there have been a few notable differences. For one thing, the number of ducks at our pond has almost doubled. Also, following the early springtime chaos, the females spent more time in the surrounding woods and brush, and the males grouped together more solidly. The males struck me as more serious and solemn as they patrolled the pond while the ducks were nesting.

And this year we have begun to see ducklings. Now the ducks always move as one. And, I should add, they continue to be capable of attacking unwanted guests. One day Ellen and I were digging holes for some pond plants, when a group of the ducks flew at us like an airplane squadron, landing just in front of our feet, in an effort to chase us from this particular spot.

Ducks swimming as a unit.

To summarize: we have given the ducks some support—daily corn and bubblers to get through the winters. But the ducks also have survived through their own initiative. They have expanded their numbers by welcoming newcomers, and they have formed an organization that is capable of chasing off geese (and threatening humans). They often patrol and act as a unit. They also have time for activities that look joyful. They still face dangers; the ducklings, in particular, are under strong predator pressure. But the ducks have come a long way from the helpless escapees who wandered alone about our farm and neighborhood. They belong to a cohesive group.

Resilient Ducks, Resilient Children

Ellen and I frequently talked about the ducks' resilience, how they overcame adversity. Ellen had a hunch that there are similarities between modes of resilience in ducks and children.

Much our understanding of children's resilience comes from research by Emmy Werner and Ruth Smith, who followed the lives of all 698 babies born in 1955 on the island of Kauai, Hawaii. Many of the children were at-risk for future problems. They grew up in poverty and frequently experienced disruptions in the family unit. Some of them had experienced birth complications and some of their parents suffered from mental illness. As the children grew up, many of the at-risk children fell into lives of crime or succumbed to mental illness. But some avoided crime and emotional illness and were coping well as adults. They held down good jobs and were involved in satisfying long-term relationships. They were happy with their lives. Werner and Smith were interested in the factors that helped these at-risk children overcome adversity.

Before I continue, I want to mention an unavoidable problem with this and other studies of resilience. To organize data, researchers must put children in categories—those who successfully adapt to adult life and those who do not. Readers might therefore infer that those in the non-resilient group are failures. But we do not really know what the individuals have gone through on a personal level. Some labeled "non-resilient" may have summoned enormous courage in the face of unbearable pressures. So the research is in this sense incomplete. Nevertheless, it can be valuable, providing insights into the kinds of activities that can help at-risk children.

A Sense of Belonging

A major Werner and Smith finding parallels my observations of the ducks: the resilient children, like the ducks, gained strength from group belonging. The children who overcame adversity participated in church groups or YMCA and YWCA organizations, raised animals in 4-H clubs, or engaged in extracurricular school activities. These children often gained support from grandparents, teachers, and close friends, and the children themselves played helpful roles in their families; they performed regular household chores and cared for younger siblings. In short, the resilient children participated in communal life and contributed to it. They gained a sense of belonging that provided them with support as they moved forward in life.

The importance of belonging isn't a new revelation. In 1930, the great French sociologist Émile Durkheim demonstrated that social solidarity buffers against depression and suicide. Although the need for belonging has been less studied in children, children do exhibit it, as when they spontaneously form clubs. You might recall creating a club in your own childhood, and smiling in recognition at Tom Sawyer's gang in *The Adventures of Huckleberry Finn*. And sometimes, if youths cannot find any sense of meaningful belonging in their communities, they create street gangs. They need to belong to something larger than themselves.

Ties to Nature

So far I have focused on the importance of *social* belonging. But there is also a sense of belonging to one's *physical environment*. Watching the ducks on the pond, I have often thought that they must feel deeply at home in the water. It is not just how they enter the water for safety that has impressed me, but the gracefulness with which they glide through it. It is impossible, of course, to know how they feel, but I imagine they experience themselves as part of it.

If children are given time in places like woods or ponds, they also can develop a sense of belonging to nature. In the preceding chapter I described how children sometimes get a feeling of oneness with all life. For example, the African American minister Howard Thurman, standing beside the ocean as a child, had the feeling of being part of everything around him. Thurman added that this feeling of oneness was a source of strength through the rest of his life. He often suffered discrimination, but society couldn't get to him because he was rooted in something far more vast—in nature or existence.

The sense of being part of nature sometimes includes other qualities. Children sometimes experience nature as if she were a good, comforting mother. Thurman, who often felt lonely as a boy, spoke this way about the night: "There was something about the night that seemed to cover my spirit like a gentle blanket. . . . [At times] I could hear the night think, and feel the night feel. This comforted me and I found myself wishing the night would hurry and come, for under its cover, my mind would roam. I felt embraced, enveloped, secure."

Children also experienced nature as a maternal presence in the Berkeley, California, schoolyard, where Robin Moore and community members replaced asphalt with soil, vegetation, and a pond—all inhabited by small animal life. In this new nature area, the students became calm and quiet, feeling comforted by their new surroundings. When asked to describe the nature area, they said things like, "It makes me feel at home." "Being alone doesn't bother me now." "It's just a good-natured place."

"It seems like one big family there." One former student, reflecting on the nature area twenty years later, likened it to a comfortable "nest." In nature, the children had found a new, loving home.

Most of us feel isolated at times. We feel alone against the world. It's therefore important to know that we have a place where we belong. After a rough day or a challenging journey, it feels good to return home. It's our port in the storm—what Mary Ainsworth called a secure home base. Knowing it is there for us, we gain confidence. These feelings of belonging may come from families or social groups or from nature. And these feelings may be a key factor in the resilience of many species, giving them the strength to carry on.

Summary

The animals on our farm sanctuary have provided me with many rewarding experiences. The animals have also prompted me to think in new ways about human children's emotions. Here is a summary of my impressions.

Fear

When we brought our first goats and sheep from the live meat market to our farm, they were extremely frightened, and during the next four weeks they hardly uttered a sound. Their silence was probably an innate response to danger. In the natural environments in which the animals evolved, noises drew the attention of nearby predators. So in times of danger, silence was highly adaptive. Because our sheep and goats had learned that humans were their killers, the animals became silent in our presence, too.

This interpretation might cast light on cases in which children become mute—a symptom that has puzzled mental health professionals. As with the sheep and goats, children's silence may be a fear reaction that emerged in our species' evolutionary past. There was a time when our species, too, had to avoid predators. True, leopards and wolf packs aren't a danger in modern life, but the ancient response of silence may still come to the fore when the child feels unprotected. I believe that psychotherapists who work with children with muteness will find it useful to consider how the children might feel unprotected.

An evolutionary perspective might clarify another puzzling behavior. In Ainsworth's widely used research situation, one-year-olds are briefly separated from their mothers, and when the mothers return, some toddlers freeze. Researchers suspect that the toddler finds the mother frightening, but they haven't seen any purpose to the freezing. They have included it in a behavior category called "disorganized/disoriented." But freezing, like silence, is a defense that many species use against predators, who rarely attack anything that stands perfectly still. Indeed, freezing is more extreme than silence, occurring when a threat is close at hand. Freezing in human children, then, may be an evolved coping mechanism in the face of immediate danger. If adults viewed freezing as the organism's attempt to survive, they might appreciate it more, and appreciation is always helpful when dealing with children.

Play

Less than ten days after he was born, our goat, Boomer, was full of playful antics. He scampered about and performed jumping stunts, climbing up a rock and jumping down at different angles. Boomer illustrates the strength of the urge to play in non-human species. So far, researchers have found playfulness in all young mammals.

Boomer's acrobatics also support a relatively new hypothesis about the adaptive value of play—that play promotes the capacity to improvise. If Boomer were to find himself in a tight spot, such as slipping from a ledge, he wouldn't panic. A creative climber and jumper, Boomer would come up with a way to leap from danger.

Human children also seem driven to play, and their play may serve the same adaptive function: it fosters the capacity to improvise. Human children, of course, not only experiment with physical actions like climbing and jumping, they also engage in symbolic play, as when they imagine themselves in various roles. But human play, too, nurtures the capacity to improvise, enabling us to meet life's challenges with creativity.

Play in human children, then, has much in common with that of other young mammals. To evolutionary theorists, this fact suggests that human children's urge to play has roots in the distant evolutionary past, in ancestors we share with other mammals. It is a contemporary continuation of a long-standing biological urge.

However, today's adults generally consider play to be unimportant—even rather frivolous. They certainly don't want playtime to interfere with academic lessons and preparation for standardized tests. I believe this curtailment of children's play is terribly misguided. Play, by promoting the capacity to innovate and improvise, has undoubtedly conferred significant survival value on our species and has become part of our genetic plan for healthy growth. To diminish it is a disservice to children and their development.

Freedom

For safety's sake, we confined our first large group of chickens to a barn and an aviary, where they were usually irritable. They made angry noises, pecked one another, and disliked humans. Then, after a few months, we decided to try giving them more freedom. We allowed them to venture into a large, adjacent pasture. As soon as they entered the pasture, they began scratching and pecking at the grass, leaves, and dirt, searching for insects. I sat on a nearby rock for an hour or so, watching their enthusiastic behavior, then I guided them back into the barn. Suddenly they were calm and contented. Since then, we have given them increasing amounts of time in pastures, and they seem to always be happy.

The change in the chickens' demeanor demonstrated the effect of freedom, but it wasn't freedom alone that made a difference. It was the freedom to engage in a natural activity—foraging—that brought them joy and fulfillment.

The chickens' behavior calls to mind Montessori's approach to education. Montessori argued that children need the freedom to choose tasks they find meaningful and learn in ways that come naturally to them. When given such tasks, children often work with great enthusiasm and concentration, and when they are finished, they are happy and serene. If similar contentment is found in other species, the findings will suggest that this response has deep biological roots, and adults will have even more reason to be on the outlook for contentment as a sign that children are growing naturally.

Care

Some of my most heartfelt moments on the farm involved Katie, a hen. Katie, who was rescued from a live meat market, went out of her way to care for a partridge and a bantam rooster, and even seemed to care about me. In the last two hours of her life, the animals in her aviary stayed close to her. It was an event unlike any I had ever seen—it was as if the other animals were holding a vigil. When I showed a video that included this event, young children in particular were deeply touched. They cried and wanted to watch it over and over. Their reactions illustrated young children's loving and caring feelings for animals.

When I talked about this topic at a conference, a former teacher, Jacqueline Pilati, told us about her experience with a class of economically disadvantaged and often-abused young children. For months, Pilati said, the children acted as if they constantly had to defend themselves and tried to solve every problem through violence. Pilati discovered that the way to unlock friendliness and compassion was by exposing them to animals. They wanted to help animals and, after that, they wanted to help other children. Other educators have independently observed that animals elicit children's caring feelings. A question for further research is whether these feelings subsequently extend to people, as happened with Pilati's pupils.

Spirituality

Natural settings sometimes produce spiritual experiences. This often occurs when the individual directly experiences nature's deep quiet or peacefulness and feels part of something larger than herself. Several careful observers believe animals have similar experiences, especially as they gaze at the horizon.

Indigenous peoples have frequently believed that animals possess a special spiritual qualilty. I suspect that the reason is that animals are so serene. Their serenity isn't limited to gazing at the horizon. I have often been impressed by the tranquililty of our sheep, goats, and other animals as they graze or forage in our pastures. What's more, their peacefulness seems to extend into the surroundings and to include me. The animals seem to have a special connection to nature's peace, which they bring to my awareness.

Among humans, it may be that children, compared to adults, more readily experience a oneness with nature and her peacefulness. Children have yet to erect firm boundaries between themselves and nature. They are more open to nature's presence, including her stillness.

Resilience

Over the hill from our sanctuary is a hunting club that ships in boxes of factory farm raised birds for its members to shoot. The birds—primarily ducks, pheasants, and partridges—stand little chance because the hunters fire at them as soon as they are released. But, miraculously, some birds escape and seek refuge on our farm or nearby. Ducks, in particular, frequently come to us. Initially, many of the ducks wandered around aimlessly and seemed helpless. But after a while the ducks organized themselves into a social group at the pond.

I was impressed by the way the ducks gained strength through group belonging, and the theme of belonging also appears in research on disadvantaged children. Werner and Smith found that those who overcame adversity benefited from participation in community activities such as church groups and YMCA and YWCA organizations. These children often gained support from grandparents, teachers, and close friends, and the children themselves played helpful roles in their families. In short, the resilient children participated in communal life and contributed to it. They gained a sense of belonging that provided them with support as they moved forward in life.

It's also possible to gain a sense of belonging to one's physical environment. Watching the grace with which ducks glide through water, I have often thought they must feel at home in it.

Children, too, can develop a sense of belonging to nature. For example, the African American minister Howard Thurman, standing beside the ocean as a child, had the feeling of being part of everything around him. Thurman added that this feeling of oneness was a source of strength through the rest of his life. He felt rooted in something very vast and profound. It is important to give all children time in nature so they have a chance to develop similar feelings.

~

PART II

Children, Animals,
and Society

~

≈ 8 ≈

Children's Sense of Closeness to Animals

I have described how human children and our farm animals share many of the same emotional behaviors. Now as I complete the preceding sentence, I fear a reaction many readers will have: "Is he saying that human children are just like animals? Isn't this demeaning to our children?"

This concern is understandable because Western culture has traditionally looked on animals as very different from and inferior to ourselves. Humans, we have been taught, are not mere animals, but higher beings. Like Spartacus in the motion picture, the heroes of many dramas proclaim their dignity with the words, "I am not an animal!"

Scholars Set Humans Apart

Scholars, too, have assumed that our species is special. Over the centuries they have asked, "What makes humans unique?" As animal researcher Alexandra Horowitz observes, those asking this question have taken it for granted that humans *are* unique. They have assumed that the only task is to identify the capacities that set us apart.

But to the consternation of many, these capacities have been hard to pinpoint. Many possibilities have seemed compelling, only to fall by the wayside. For example, scientists once believed that humans are the only species that makes tools. But in 1960 Jane Goodall found that chimpanzees also do so. They strip the leaves off twigs, and then poke the twigs down holes to fish for termites. Since then, crows and dolphins have been observed making simple tools, too. Humans, of course, invent more advanced tools, but tool-making isn't uniquely human.

In addition, the capacities for language, culture, symbol use, and altruism were once considered to be uniquely human but have been found in other animals. Nevertheless, the search continues. There must be *something*, people assume, that explains our clear superiority. We're not mere animals.

Some scientists concede that other animals possess most human capacities but say that we humans are really on a different plane because our capacities are light-years more advanced. This often seems to be the case—until a researcher looks very carefully and openly at what an animal can actually do.

A case in point is Karl von Frisch's classic research on the humble honey bee. Prior to his studies, in the mid-20th century, no one suspected the extent of the bees' communicative powers. Because von Frisch's work is so eye-opening, I will take a moment to summarize it before moving on to the main topic of this chapter, which is the child's feelings about animals.

Honey Bees

Near the end of their lives, worker bees (who are always female) are given the task of searching for food, pollen, and other resources. A bee's expeditions often take her three or four miles from the hive. On occasion, she may travel over six miles. When she returns to the hive with whatever she has found, she conveys important information to the other worker bees. She does this by means of a dance she performs on the surface of the honeycomb, deep inside the hive.

One message is the desirability of the resource, based on the current needs of the colony. If, for example, she has discovered a rich source of nectar, and the colony badly needs it, she will dance very energetically, and several others will replicate her journey.

The dancing bee also indicates the distance to the resource by the duration of a segment of her dance. But most impressively, she "diagrams" the direction that the others must travel. If she dances straight up the wall of the honeycomb, it means, "When you go outside the hive, fly exactly in the direction of the sun." If she dances straight down, it means, "Fly opposite the direction of the sun." If she dances along an angle, such as 45 degrees to the right of a straight-up vertical, this means, "Go 45 degrees to the right of the sun." Whatever the correct angle, her dance communicates it.

When von Frisch's findings became known, many psychologists minimized their importance. A major psychology textbook said, "You and I can have endless conversations about all sorts of subjects, but bees are able to discuss one thing only—food and where to find it." This is wrong. In addition to the location of food (nectar and pollen), bees also convey information on where to find water, resin, and possible new hive sites. They also hold collective gatherings at which they seem to debate the relative merits of new hive sites. Admittedly, human communication is broader than bee communication. Some humans will talk about anything, even imaginary things. But it is telling how the textbook significantly underestimated the range of honey bee communication.

Moreover, psychologists and other scientists have been slow to acknowledge the bees' high level of symbolic representation. It strikes me that the bees' dance is similar to the mental activity of ship officers who gather inside a cabin to chart their voyage on the open sea. Using a protractor and other instruments, the officers draw the desired trajectory on a map. Few would question that an advanced form of symbolic representation is involved. And when a honey bee, deep inside the hive, provides a kind of vector map that shows others where to fly, her symbolic representation seems just as advanced. But scientists have been slow to recognize that a small insect could share such high-level symbolic activity with human beings, whom the scientists deem to be infinitely superior. Once again, I recognize that humans can apply symbolic communication across a much wider range of topics, but the bee's symbolic activity is closer to that of mature humans than scientists have generally acknowledged.

The Child's More Inclusive View

Children, in contrast, do not set themselves apart from the animals. They view animals as similar to themselves and feel a kinship with them.

Among the first to notice this childhood attitude was Sigmund Freud. In *Totem and Taboo*, Freud wrote, "Children show no trace of the arrogance which urges adult civilized men to draw a hard-and-fast line between their own nature and that of all other animals. Children have no scruples over allowing animals to rank as their full equals."

Albert Schweitzer recalled how he, as a boy, was puzzled by this "hard-and-fast line" that adults draw.

"It was quite incomprehensible to me—this was before I began going to school—why in my evening prayers I should pray for human beings only. So when my mother had prayed with me and I had kissed her good night, I used to add silently a prayer that I composed myself for all living creatures."

The pioneering developmental scholar Jean Piaget observed that young children have a feeling of communion with animals and talk to them. Children say things like, "Good-bye cow," and, "What are you up to, grasshopper?" Marie Rose Mukeni Beya, a psychologist who raised her children in the Congo, told me that when her son was four years old he asked his dog to join him in his prayers. "It was hard to believe," Beya said, "but the dog actually sat still as if he were praying."

Should One Invite Animals to a Party?

Stimulated by theses anecdotes, I wondered if young children in New York City might be more inclined than older children to include animals in social events. In an informal pilot study, psychology students Carolina Franco and Keyonna Hayes and I individually conducted brief interviews with a small number of young children. The children were predominantly from African American and Latino families. We presented each child with small dolls—a boy and a girl doll, and a sheep and a horse doll—and asked, "This girl and boy want to have a party. They are thinking about inviting the sheep and the horse. Is that a good idea?"

We interviewed eleven three- to five-year-olds. Most of them (eight of the eleven) said yes, the children should invite the animals to the party. They explained that the animals "want to go," and "are nice," and "it's fun." One three-year-old added that "the sheep wants to be with the boy."

Our seven and eight year olds responded differently. Most of these children (seven of the eight) believed that inviting the animals to a party was a bad idea. They explained that "the animals would destroy the house and make a mess," "Animals don't go to parties," "It's not normal," and "They are animals, and I didn't see any animals at the weddings and parties I went to with my dad."

If these age trends hold up in larger samples (with a broader array of questions), the results would suggest that younger children are, indeed, more inclusive in their attitudes toward animals. Older children, in contrast, seem to be picking up the social norms that draw a sharp line between the activities of humans and animals. Humans go to parties; animals do not.

Is There Value in Loose Boundaries?

Many developmental psychologists view human/animal boundaries from another perspective. They see human/

animal distinctions as among the many that the child makes as she develops her individual personality.

This process starts in infancy. Initially, many psychologists believe, infants possess little sense of themselves apart from their mothers or caretakers. Once they have developed self/caretaker boundaries, they have taken a significant step forward.

But their boundaries are far from complete. As Piaget observed, children still fail to separate themselves from the outside world in important ways. Prior to the age of six or seven years, children typically assume that physical objects such as clouds, wind, the sun, and even stones are alive and think and feel just like they do. Piaget referred to this childhood view as "animistic." As the child develops, she distinguishes between herself, a thinking, feeling human, from the world of inert, physical objects. She also begins to distinguish humans from plants and animals.

Piaget and many others have assumed that such distinctions represent unequivocal progress. The self becomes less confused with the rest of the world. Piaget and others have noted that indigenous peoples tend to be animistic, but the scholars have dismissed animism as primitive.

However, a few contemporary writers, including Theodore Roszak and David Abram, believe animism is needed today. In Western societies, they say, we have become extremely shut off from the natural world. We view nature as inert matter or statistical units and have lost touch with nature's expressive qualities. Fortunately, even in our society there are some who retain the child's openness to the ways in which nature shares our emotional expression. These are poets and other artists.

Poets, for example, may say that the wind whispers, thunder explodes with anger, and a brook sings with joy. And through their poems, they help us experience the world more vividly.

Jane Goodall's Approach

Although she is known as a scientist, Jane Goodall exhibited animistic attitudes, especially when she began her studies of wild chimpanzees in 1960. Each day, Goodall climbed up hills in the Gombe forest to try to catch glimpses of the chimps. The chimps avoided people, so much of the time Goodall was alone. However, she experienced the forest as a living presence. Each day she said "Good morning" to a peak and a spring, and she perceived emotions such as tempestuousness in a strong wind and eagerness in a young sapling's growth. Goodall's animistic experiences might seem fanciful, immature, or simply the product of loneliness, but they reveal the extent to which she was open to the vitality and expressiveness of the forest.

Moreover, when she finally gained the chimpanzees' trust and was able to observe them in detail, she was fully open to their personal traits and all the thoughts and emotions they might have. This openness violated the scientific canon of her day. Only humans were credited with individual personalities, thoughts, and emotions. To speak of these qualities in animals was to commit the sin of anthropomorphism. Animals were supposed to be treated only as numbers. But Goodall had not studied at a university yet and didn't know about this taboo. Instead, she named the chimpanzees and was open to the possibility that they could think and feel just like she could.

And because she erected no sharp boundary between herself and the chimpanzees, she discovered that they did, indeed, possess a wealth of human traits.

> The more I learned, the more I realized how like us they were in so many ways. I observed how they could reason and plan for the immediate future. . . . And then there were the postures and gestures that complemented the sounds they made—their communication repertoire. Many of these were common to human cultures around the world—kissing, embracing, holding hands, patting one another on the back, swaggering . . . I gradually learned about the long-term affectionate and supportive bonds between family members and close friends. I also learned that they could bear grudges.

Even when Goodall found out that scientific conventions required her to place an intellectual barrier between herself and the chimpanzees, she refused to do so. She remained receptive to the full range of their cognitive and emotional behavior, and continued to make many discoveries.

Heightened Spiritual States

In 1902, the philosopher and psychologist William James wrote about spiritual experiences in which people feel a heightened closeness—a oneness, actually—with animals and nature. As we saw in Chapter 5, such experiences are present in children. In fact, they may be more common in children than in adults. With porous boundaries between the self and nature, children seem more prone to enter states in which they feel a unity with their natural surroundings. Often, they feel included in nature's deep peacefulness. For example, we saw how Gladys Corunna, an Aboriginal Australian, found relief from an unhappy childhood by going to a special place where she watched the water gurgle over the rocks and listened to the birds. After a while, Corunna said, "The peace of that place would enter into me."

As children grow up, they often have difficulty recapturing a sense of oneness with nature. As poets such as Wordsworth and Whittier have observed, people become integrated into a Western culture that closes them off from their natural surroundings. But a small percentage of people somehow retain their childhood openness to the natural world and continue to feel states of oneness with her. Jane Goodall exemplifies this pattern.

As a child, Goodall spent hours sitting in the branches of her favorite tree. "There, high above the ground, I could feel a part of the life of the tree." When, several years later, she studied the chimpanzees in the Gombe forest, she had other intense experiences. For example, one afternoon after a strong rain, she became lost in the beauty around her and says, "I must have slipped into a state of heightened awareness. . . . It seemed to me, as I struggled afterward to recall the experience, that *self* was absent: I and the chimpanzees, the earth and trees and air, seemed to merge, to become one with the spirit power of earth itself." Such experiences included a sense of inner calm. She felt the peace of the forest within her.

Goodall has been open to the possibility that chimpanzees, too, enter spiritual states. Specifically, she has described how the Gombe chimps expressed awe at the sight of a waterfall. But as I mentioned in Chapter 5, nothing similar has been observed by other investigators. In contrast, a number of observers have noted that animals gazing at the horizon, or just foraging, seem to feel part of a deep peacefulness in the world. It is this kind of experience that human children, compared to adults, seem particularly capable of having.

Ethics

In the opening pages of E.B. White's *Charlotte's Web*, the farmer, Mr. Arable, is about to kill a runt piglet. But his eight-year-old daughter, Fern, intervenes, grabbing his axe handle to stop him. Mr. Arable explains that a runt makes trouble for the farm, but Fern shouts, "It's unfair."

> "If I had been very small at birth, would you have killed me?"
>
> Mr. Arable smiled. "Certainly not," he said, looking down at his daughter with love. "But this is different. A little girl is one thing, a little runty pig is another."
>
> "I see no difference," replied Fern, still hanging on to the ax. "This is the most terrible case of injustice I ever heard of."

Fern's viewpoint differs radically from the ethics of most Western philosophers, who haven't seen the need to include animals in their ethical considerations. Even Immanuel Kant, widely considered the greatest of moral philosophers, said that people have no moral obligations to animals. Fern, however, argues that justice applies to animals as well as humans. She sees "no difference" between herself and the little pig.

Do children really think like Fern?

The most relevant studies have been conducted by University of Washington psychologist Peter Kahn, who has asked children in the United States, Brazil, and Portugal about events such as pollution and oil spills. Kahn has found that almost all children are very concerned about these events, primarily because of the danger they present to humans. But by the fifth grade (and sometimes as early as the third grade), some children argue that the natural environment—and animals in particular—have value in their own right. The children say animals have rights and deserve respect.

Kahn notes that such responses are usually in the minority, but many researchers would be surprised by the early age at which these responses appear. Psychologist Lawrence Kohlberg concluded that discussions of rights and respect for others involve high levels of reasoning and rarely emerge prior to late adolescence, if then. Perhaps when children speak in defense of animals, their passions spur them to unusually high levels of thinking. In any case, the children who call attention to animals' rights frequently emphasize that animals and humans are basically the same.

One example in Kahn's interviews is a boy named Arnold, a fifth grader who lived in an impoverished section of Houston. Arnold decried the effects of pollution on fish because "fish need the same respect as we need." Justifying his arguments, Arnold pointed to similarities between fish and humans: "They don't have noses, but they have scales to breathe, and they have mouths like we have mouths. . . . Fishes, they want to live freely, just like we live freely. . . . They don't like living in an environment where there is so much pollution that they die every day."

Arnold went on to assert that "every animal deserves respect." Kahn asked him if this included mosquitoes. Arnold laughed and said, "Well, not really. Because mosquitoes they begin to get on your nerves a little bit. And they make little bumps on you. . . . But it's still wrong to kill 'em though. Because they really need to live freely too, just like every insect, every bear, any kind of type of human . . ."

Other children in Kahn's interviews also pointed to fundamental similarities between humans and other animals. They said things such as, "They're . . . living things just like we are. You wouldn't want anybody to kill you like that," and, "Just because [fish] can't talk, they're animals, and I don't think that's right, they could be people if they could talk, a form of people, well not human beings but something like it." A Brazilian child (a fifth grader) said it's wrong for birds to die from pollution, "Because birds have a life as we do, they have a mother, they are like us."

⇜ 9 ⇝

Becoming Detached

"Where has our empathy gone?" —MELANIE JOY

⌒

A t the beginning of the 20th century, several psychologists kept diaries of their children's' conversations.
One British diarist, James Sully, reported a conversation
between his four-year-old son and his mother in which
the boy became upset. He was looking at a picture book
and asked his mother why people kill stags. She said it
was because people like to chase them.

> Child: Why don't the police stop them?
>
> Mother: They can't do that, because people are
> allowed to kill them.
>
> Child (loudly and passionately): Allowed, allowed?
> People are not allowed to take other people and
> kill them.
>
> Mother: People think there is a difference between
> killing men and killing animals.

Child (was not to be pacified this way. He looked woe-begone, and said to his mother piteously): You don't understand me.

Although this conversation took place in England over a century ago, it illustrates a conflict that is very much with us in the United States today. The young child, who cares deeply about animals, grows up in a society of adults who are largely indifferent. Most US adults eat meat, tolerate sport hunting, and don't lose sleep over the condition of animals in zoos, rodeos, circuses, or research labs. They care about pets, but few other species. In fact, when it comes to today's most widespread animal suffering—that on factory farms—adult knowledge has been quite limited. This, at least, is what a Wesleyan psychology professor found in brief surveys in the early 1990s and what my undergraduate research students and I found more recently.

From December 2005 to April 2011, three of my students (Srushti Vanjari, David Kremelberg, and Mauricio Toussant) and I distributed very brief questionnaires that asked, "How much knowledge do you have about the factory farms that raise animals for food?" People were asked to check off either "A great deal," "A good amount," "A slight amount," or "None." We distributed the questionnaires in student commons or gathering places at five colleges (The City College of New York, Columbia University, the University of California San Diego, Valencia Community College in Orlando, Florida, and the University of Miami). We also distributed the questionnaires in two hotel lobbies and a senior citizens center in the New York City metropolitan area. Our sample totaled 433 respondents. We chose a hotel that was expensive and another that was inexpensive to tap different social strata.

In all but one of these samples, the overwhelming majority of individuals—73 to 90 percent—rated their knowledge of factory farms as either slight or nonexistent. The exception was Columbia University, which has a reputation for radical student politics. There, almost half the students estimated their knowledge to be more substantial. But, overall, our respondents reported that they didn't know much about factory farms.

Admittedly, our surveys are informal, and most of my colleagues have a different impression. They believe that people have become very aware of the treatment of farmed animals and many people have adopted vegetarian diets. This also has been the impression of some popular writers. For example, in his 2006 book *The Omnivore's Dilemma*, Michael Pollan wrote, "Vegetarianism is more popular than it has ever been, and animal rights, the fringiest of fringe movements until just a few years ago, is rapidly finding its way into the cultural mainstream." Actually, in 2008, two years after Pollan's book appeared, a Harris poll found that only 3.2 percent of US adults followed a vegetarian diet, and only half of those did so out of a concern for animals' welfare. In 2011 and 2012, Harris and Gallup polls, respectively, revealed that the 3.2 percent figure had risen to 5 percent—hardly a mass movement.

It is possible that the dramatic attitude shifts that Pollan and others believed they saw did actually materialize after 2012. But we need data—not general impressions—to know. And it's quite possible that a large majority of adult Americans will continue to view animal suffering with detachment—to the extent they know about it at all.

What is it like to be a child in such a society? How might our society produce the detachment that's so prevalent in adulthood? Unfortunately, there is little research on these questions, but I'll sketch out the picture that has emerged so far.

The Young Child's Rude Awakening

A critical event occurs in the early childhood years, when children discover the source of the meat they eat. In a small study of twenty-eight urban, middle class children, one of my undergraduate students, Alina Pavlakos, found that most five-year-olds didn't know where meat comes from. They knew they ate meat, but when asked, "Do you eat animals?" most said, "*Nooo!*"—as if the idea were outrageous.

Pavlakos found that children soon learn otherwise, most by the age of six. She and others also have informally observed that many children become distraught when they learn the facts. As Jane Goodall and Peter Singer have pointed out, some children want to become vegetarians at this point, but their parents rarely permit it. The developmental psychologist Lawrence Kohlberg, who usually championed children's independent thinking, spent six months persuading his young son to abandon vegetarianism. It will be important to learn more about what goes on in five- and six-year-olds' minds at this point, when the children encounter the conventional adult attitudes toward food.

Middle Childhood:
The Loss of Nature Exploration

Developmental psychologists refer to the next several years, from about seven to twelve, as "middle childhood." Broadly speaking, the child's mind is different from that of the younger child. It is less prone to fantasy and is more logical and realistic. Because children are more sensible, parents have traditionally allowed them to spend more time away from direct parental supervision.

If you grew up in the 1940s, '50s, or '60s, you probably remember this age of childhood as a time of outdoor adventure. You might have ridden your bike around the neighborhood to see who was outside, climbed fences to explore vacant lots, or walked down to the pond to see what was there. During these explorations, you probably encountered birds, insects, frogs, and small mammals. Although research on such adventures is rather sparse, it seems that the child's interest in nature and animals is quite strong. As Edith Cobb wrote in a classic 1959 essay, "The natural world is experienced in some highly evocative way." Then, with the onset of adolescence, this interest generally wanes. The teenager is more concerned with his or her status in the social world of peers.

If, during the middle childhood years, children can actively explore nature, their attachment to nature and animals can grow. As I mentioned in Chapter 6, this occurred in the Berkeley elementary schoolyard. When Robin Moore and his coworkers replaced asphalt with a nature area, the children loved to observe the animals and developed caring attitudes toward them.

But the Berkeley project was a rare event in modern American life. It provided children with personal contact with nature when powerful economic and social forces were already reducing this contact. By the time of the Berkeley project, in the 1970s, real estate development had destroyed many of the vacant lots, woods, and ponds that children loved to explore. In addition, the phenomenal popularity of TV had drawn children indoors. More recently, the lure of the Internet and video games has added to the time children spend looking at screens. Parents also have become increasingly hesitant to allow their children to play freely out-of-doors, because the parents fear kidnappers and other dangers. And even when children do go outdoors, they increasingly focus on their hand-held smart phones, rather than the world around them.

All these trends have combined to dramatically reduce modern children's personal experiences with nature and animals. The decline of family farms also has contributed to this effect. True, children still have pets. But children's experiences with animals are otherwise limited. Most of their information comes from the media.

TV commercials bombard children with the message that happy families eat lots of meat, although the commercials rarely spell out where the meat comes from. TV nature shows provide more specific information about *wild* animals, and movies such as *Free Willy* and *Babe* reaffirm children's affection for animals. But the media's positive depictions of animals are not supplemented by real-life experiences. Children rarely observe actual animals caring for their babies, and children rarely rescue and care for injured animals. Lacking such personal experiences, children's affection for animals fails to develop as strongly as it could. And when children become adults, and can more freely make their own dietary choices, they lack a childhood reservoir of affection to guide them.

I am not suggesting that if children had more personal contact with animals, as in days-gone-by, they would love animals so deeply they would all become vegetarians. Children in earlier times ate meat, and they grew into adults who did so. I am only suggesting that more personal experience with animals would strengthen feelings for animals among many children. Then, when they heard about the extreme cruelty of today's factory farms, their childhood feelings for animals would come to the fore and they would be more inclined to oppose the abuse.

Detachment Mechanisms

Still, the suffering of animals on factory farms (as well as in research labs and other conditions) can be so awful that many adults, whatever their childhood experiences, might become upset if they knew what the animals go through. Unfortunately for the animals, our society has ways of limiting what people know and blunting their emotional reactions. It keeps them detached. In the paragraphs that follow, I discuss some of these "detachment mechanisms." My discussion draws on my personal observations as well as those of writers such as Peter Singer, John Robbins, Scott Plous, and Melanie Joy.

Media Filters

One reason that it is difficult for us to know much about factory farms is that they are almost all located in isolated, rural parts of the country. Even so, the media might bring the factory farms into our homes, but it has been slow to do so. Except for an occasional late-night cable documentary, it's rare to see footage of animals on factory farms on television or in motion pictures. As Melanie Joy says, "Most of us know more about what the stars wore to the Oscars than we do about the animals we eat."

Similarly, the print media often assumes that the animals on factory farms are relatively unimportant. This has been true of the prestigious newspaper *The New York Times*. After the November 2008 elections, the *Times* listed the results of "major ballot measures." The list included referenda on the legalization of small amounts of marijuana in Massachusetts and Michigan, and a declaration that English be the official language of government agencies in Missouri. But the list didn't mention the California ballot initiative that eventually will ease the confinement of pigs and chickens.

To be sure, the *Times* has written editorials deploring the current practices of factory farms. Between 2002 and 2011, I counted six such editorials. In four of the six, the editors focused on the side effects of the industry, especially the effects of large quantities of manure and antibiotics on human health. These four editorials said *nothing* about the lives of the animals. It often seems that animals aren't sufficiently important to merit the attention of America's "paper of record."

Language

In several cases, our language hides the identity of our food. We eat pork, not pigs; veal, not calves; meat, not flesh. The killing of wildlife, too, is disguised. Wildlife managers and hunters say a person "takes" or "harvests" deer, bears, and wild birds. They rarely say a person actually "kills" an animal.

The 19th century philosopher Arthur Schopenhauer pointed out that the English language has a more subtle way of distancing us from animals. Our language does this by referring to animals with the impersonal pronoun "it," as if animals were mere objects. The personal pronoun "who" is incorrect. Our language forces us to use the words that imply that an animal is a thing—not a living being.

Denial

It's not just the media and our language that hide the suffering of animals from us. We also hide it from ourselves. Many of us would rather not learn about the treatment of animals, especially when it might spoil our meals. As John Robbins observes, intelligent people will say, "Don't tell me what happens to the animals. It will spoil my dinner."

I screened this knowledge from myself for many years, as I mentioned in the beginning of this book. When a vague concern about the source of meat entered my mind, I pushed it aside. And after I became a vegetarian, I found that many people considered it rude to even bring the topic up.

Robbins refers to our wish to look away as "repression" and "denial." These are defense mechanisms in psychoanalytic theory, and of the two, denial more accurately describes what occurs in the case of animal suffering. Most of the time, people try to keep from looking at the facts. However, in psychoanalytic theory, defense mechanisms work unconsciously, beneath our awareness. When people consciously defend themselves against knowledge, then, it's not pure denial, but a kind of "conscious denial."

Statistics and Abstractions

As Jonathan Balcombe and Melanie Joy point out, our society also distances us from animals by considering them as population statistics rather than as individuals. Population statistics are more impersonal, so we can more readily tolerate animals' deaths when we consider them on this level.

This is very true in the case of fish, who are increasingly raised in factory farm conditions, crowded together so tightly that they can barely move. In government documents, fish are not discussed as individuals, but as quantifiable stocks, resources, and yields. Reading the documents, one would hardly know that they were talking about individual fish at all. It's as if fishing industries merely affect numbers—hardly something that tugs at anyone's heartstrings.

Even The Safina Center (formerly the Blue Ocean Institute), which seeks to defend fish, discusses fish as population statistics. The Safina Center asks us to avoid eating fish such as Atlantic halibut and bluefin tuna primarily because their numbers are in peril. The Center recommends that we eat fish such as Atlantic pollock and chub mackerel because these fish stocks are at healthy levels. But what about the individual fish? Each fish pulled from the sea writhes and gasps for oxygen. Each wants to live.

The reduction of animals to numbers pervades sport hunting. Documents such as New Jersey's 2010 *Comprehensive Black Bear Management Policy* speak of "population reduction" and "desired densities." When, in 2003, the State of New Jersey introduced its first black bear hunt in thirty-three years, a *New York Times* editorial backed the hunt as necessary to "thin their ranks," adding that the hunt was unlikely to "endanger the bear population." If, however, we think of each bear as an individual, it's not so easy to endorse the killing. For each particular bear is a living, breathing, feeling being—whose life is about to be taken away.

It is especially easy to think of animals who live in groups—such as deer, cattle, and chickens—as statistics rather than as individuals because they strike us as so similar. But as Balcombe emphasizes, members of such species do have individual personalities. Farmers have long known this, and avoid giving animals individual names because it makes it more difficult to slaughter them. Joy adds that "countless students of mine . . . have reported that after getting to know an individual 'food' animal, they felt unable to consume that particular animal, and some even felt uncomfortable continuing to eat meat from that species." But aside from pets, most people today have little personal contact with animals, so they don't get to know them as individuals.

We also distance ourselves from animals by keeping discussions on a theoretical plane. A case in point is Richard Louv's 2005 book, *Last Child in the Woods*. This book has done more than any other to raise public awareness about children's alienation from nature. Louv wants children to have direct experience with nature and develop reverence for it. But in the course of the book Louv defends hunting and fishing. Although these sports do provide children with firsthand experience with nature, it's difficult to see how killing an animal for sport shows reverence for the animal. To defend his position, Louv moves to the abstract intellectual level. When it comes to fishing, Louv says the central question is whether fish feel pain and suffer, and the answer "depends on your definition of pain and suffering." Louv chooses not to delve into the question, but adds that the answer "is not so clear as it may seem. Certainly, the definition is not settled." So what seems straightforward to us when we watch a fish gasping for oxygen becomes a matter of abstract definition—and therefore removed from our emotional response.

Detachment as an Ideological Tool

Melanie Joy proposes that the above kinds of detachment mechanisms serve a dominant ideology she calls "carnism." Carnism maintains that violence toward animals is ethical and acceptable. As an ideology, carnism is unusual because it is largely invisible. People are not aware that meat-eating reflects values; they simply see it as normal and natural. Most people don't realize that they have been taught to value human life so far above that of other animals that it's acceptable to eat them. If, Joy adds, carnism were to be openly examined, it would fall apart. So it relies on detachment mechanisms to keep itself intact. It survives because we see animals as things and statistics and avoid thinking about the animal suffering we are supporting. Carnism functions like the cinematic Matrix, a mental prison that prevents us from perceiving reality.

Can We Readily Overcome Detachment?

Joy suggests that this mental system is actually quite fragile: "Carnism is like the Wizard of Oz; once the curtain is pulled back from the system, its power virtually disappears." But I don't think it's this easy. Two strong motives make it difficult for us to "pull the curtain," to open ourselves to animals' plight. The first motive stems from our capacity for empathy.

As John Robbins suggests, if we open ourselves to animal suffering, we cannot help from sharing some of their pain. Because of our natural empathy, we hurt, too. Robbins adds that we suffer because we are not separate from animals: "Our pain arises from our kinship with life." It is more comfortable to look the other way.

When we do open ourselves to animal suffering, we usually try to do something about it. Most often, we decide to try a vegetarian diet. But this decision brings a second motive into play—the need for belonging. Vegetarianism becomes difficult because it separates us from the customs of our families, friends, and the mainstream society.

In his book, *The Omnivore's Dilemma*, Michael Pollan described his own difficulty making this separation. As part of his investigation of meat-eating in our society, he decided to try out vegetarianism himself. He wrote, "Healthy and virtuous as I may feel these days, I also feel alienated from traditions I value: cultural traditions like the Thanksgiving turkey, or even franks at the ballpark, and family traditions like my mother's beef brisket at Passover. These ritual meals link us to our history along multiple lines—family, religion, landscape, [and] nation. . . ." Pollan's feeling of cultural isolation affected him deeply; after his experiment with vegetarianism, he resumed eating meat.

Although I wish Pollan had stuck with vegetarianism, I agree that the need for social belonging is powerful. As I discussed in the first section of this book, my own need to belong to the mainstream society delayed my decision to come to the aid of animals.

After spending time with the animals on our farm, I also became more aware of belonging's positive side. In particular, the ducks on our pond gave me a new appreciation of how individuals can often accomplish more as a group than they can alone. Then, with my observations of the ducks in mind, I saw how disadvantaged children, too, benefit from group belonging. A feeling of social support can give all of us confidence and energy. Perhaps people who want to defend animals can turn this fact to their advantage. Perhaps they can develop groups and social ties that will provide them with new strength, making it easier to work on animals' behalf.

Nevertheless, for the immediate future most support groups will be new and small and will have to to compete with the powerful effects of our social upbringing. As children, almost all of us were raised by families and a society-at-large that routinely consumed animal products. Perhaps we had misgivings as young children, but we grew up taking it for granted that meat-eating is normal. And, as psychologist Ernest Schachtel emphasized, our embeddedness in social conventions has given us a deep sense of security. To venture outside conventions can be frightening. How is it possible to do so?

≈ 10 ≈

Going Forward

Those who wish to defend animals need a new value system. Venturing into relatively uncharted waters, they need at least the beginnings of guiding principles and ideas. When talking to friends, writing letters to editors, or testifying at public hearings, they need to be able to give some explanation of why it's right to defend animals. Of equal importance, people need values that feel right to them, on the inside.

As a profession, discussions of principles and values have been the task of philosophers. But in Western philosophy, animals have been largely excluded from the moral discourse.

Albert Schweitzer likened Western moral philosophy to a person who has just scrubbed a floor and doesn't want the family dog to walk on it and mark it up. Philosophers, Schweitzer said, don't want animals "to wander about in their fields of ethics."

This point was driven home to me as a new member of our college's faculty senate, in 1990. The senate was debating a proposal to install a monkey research lab. At one point, a distinguished English professor rose to say that no one had explained why any ethical considerations should extend beyond human beings. Why should we give animals any moral status? "Unless this is explained," he said, "I will vote for the monkey lab."

I searched my mind for a good response; I tried to remember what moral philosophers had to say about assigning moral status to animals. But nothing significant came to mind. Since then, I've found that a handful of contemporary philosophers have tried to explain why we should include animals in moral deliberations. Sometimes they have drawn on the thoughts of an even smaller number of earlier philosophers. So far, I believe the most compelling argument is made by Peter Singer. Singer emphasizes that other animals, like us, experience pain, and if we believe we have a moral obligation to reduce suffering in the world, we must include animals. To ignore their suffering, and focus only on our own species, is self-serving and prejudicial.

As we think about a more inclusive moral philosophy, it's important to keep an eye on biological and animal behavior research. Microbiologists have found that all species essentially use the same genetic code and synthesize proteins from the same amino acids. In addition, the monumental research on genomes—total DNA sequences—has revealed stunning similarities across species. Meanwhile, animal behavior researchers find increasing evidence that other species share, at least to some extent, human cognitive and emotional capacities. More and more, it appears that all species are related, as Darwin proposed. We all belong to one extended family. It may be helpful for government officials and the public to know that when misery is inflicted on animals, it is inflicted on their relatives.

The Wisdom of Children

As people attempt to move beyond society's dominant views of animals, they can also draw on a neglected idea that goes back to ancient times. This is the view that there is a special wisdom in the child's ways of knowing. This view is found in the ancient Chinese Taoist statement, "Wise souls are children." This view is also present in Western thought, especially in the Rousseauist or Romantic tradition. Writers such as Ernest Schachtel, Abraham Maslow, and David Abram, and poets such as William Wordsworth and John Greenleaf Whittier, have called attention to children's open fascination with nature and their feeling for it. Children do not place themselves apart from nature, but experience it with an instinctive empathy. As a result, nature is full of richness and vitality. Sadly, Romantic writers say, adult society gets its hooks into children and teaches them to detach themselves from nature. It teaches them to see much of life as impersonal matter and statistical information. The natural world becomes more objective, but it is no longer a source of wonder.

Based on the accounts I have given in this book, this Romantic view seems quite accurate with respect to animals. Early on, children take a loving interest in animals and want to protect them. They do not regard animals as fundamentally different from themselves, but feel a kinship with them. In their moral reasoning, they sometimes make impressive comments about other animals' commonalities with humans.

For animal defenders, the childhood attitudes offer encouragement. They indicate that a strong affinity to animals is part of our nature, existing before the socialization process disrupts it. It is a basic resource we can try to regain. Wordsworth expressed this hope in his great poem, "Ode: Intimations of Immortality." He felt that although we can never fully recover our childhood vision of nature's glory, the early feelings for nature aren't totally lost.

> Though nothing can bring back the hour
> Of splendour in the grass, of glory in the flower;
> We will grieve not, rather find
> Strength in what remains behind;
> In the primal sympathy
> Which having been must ever be

I have found that it can be helpful to call attention to this bond—this "primal sympathy"—when trying to convince public bodies to halt wildlife hunts and culls. I have often said something like, "I know I have a chance to convince you to halt this plan to kill animals because there was a time when you yourself were an animal rights advocate. This is when you were a child. You once loved animals very much and would have hated to see harm come to them. So deep inside, you all have feelings for animals."

I ask the audience to consider their childhood feelings as valid—indeed, as more honest than all they've been taught about human superiority. This approach doesn't completely change minds, but it does get people to listen.

Finally, I would like to call attention to my most surprising observation: Animals seem capable of spiritual experiences. Goats, dogs, seagulls, and perhaps many other animals gaze across the horizon and receive a sense of deep peace in the world—an experience that has been called mystical. Animals are also often very calm when grazing, and they might feel nature's peace at these times, too. Although it's just a tentative possibility, animals' capacity to feel nature's serenity might actually be greater than ours. This is important because regardless of the continuities researchers find between humans and other species, it always seems that people can say, "Yes, there's a similarity, but the human capacity is so much greater." For example, people can say that although bees can communicate through symbols, human symbolic communication covers a broader range of topics. Whereas bees communicate about their colony resource needs, humans communicate about anything, including imaginary topics. Whatever the capacity, people seem to find a way of defending a hierarchy that keeps animals beneath us. But in the case of spirituality, the capacity of animals may actually turn out to be greater than ours. (Some might say they are closer to God.) And if so, many people will feel that animals deserve much more respect than they are usually accorded.

The poet Rainer Maria Rilke took a strong interest in this topic. In his "Eighth Elegy," Rilke wrote that the free animal "looks out into the Open," which is actually the eternal. At these times, Rilke speculated, the animal feels that her life is "boundless," for the animal is part of the vastness she experiences. There are no boundaries. Humans, in contrast, rarely experience the world so profoundly. Instead, they stand apart from it, perceiving only specific objects.

The main exception, Rilke added, is the young child, who can enter the same open vastness as the animal does. A child "may wander there for hours, through the timeless stillness," and "may get lost in it." But the adult society doesn't allow the child to linger. It shakes the child back into the world of distinct objects that are separate from her.

As we have seen, there is some evidence, though still preliminary, that childhood is indeed a time when humans are especially prone to lose themselves in nature's "timeless stillness." One task we might set for ourselves, then, is to allow children more free time in natural settings so they can have such experiences. Moreover, we might resolve to become more like children ourselves. Children may be our best link to the animals' deep sense of peace in the world. In this sense, Wordsworth may have been right to identify the child as "Nature's Priest."

Notes

Introduction, My Decision to Defend Animals

PAGE

xvii Bowlby's work: Bowlby 1982; Crain 2011, Ch. 3.

xviii Ainsworth's patterns of attachment: Crain 2011, Ch. 3.

xx Search for human uniqueness: Horowitz 2009.

xx Animals make tools: Goodall 2003, 66–67; Gazzaniga 2008, 45.

xx Animals use symbols. See, for example, research on bee communication: von Frisch 1967; Griffin 1992, Ch. 9.

xx Animals transmit culture: Vaidyanathan 2011.

xx Resistance to evolutionary psychology: Kenrick 2010; Cosmides and Tooby 2010.

xx Examples of evolutionary psychology's emphasis on human uniqueness: Pinker and Bloom 1992; Dunbar, Barrett, and Lycett 2007, Chs. 4, 8–10.

xx For a thoughtful account of research by the minority who explore animal roots of human behavior, see Bekoff and Pierce 2009.

xxi "To see what there is": Lorenz 1971, 129.

xxi Ethologists want to observe animals in the wild: Lorenz 1981, 47-53; Hess 1962, 160.

Chapter 1, Fear

6 Lorenz recommends study in the wild: Lorenz 1981, 47–53.

8 Ainsworth's experimental situation: Crain 2011, 60.

8 Behavior researchers couldn't classify: Main and Solomon 1990.

8 Most common "disorganized" behaviors are averting head and freezing: see Lyons-Ruth and Jacobvitz 2008, 668; Main and Solomon 1990.

8 Main and Solomon concluded children "lack a strategy": Main and Solomon 1990; see also Lyons-Ruth and Jacobvitz 2008, 667.

9 Found in 14 to 24 percent of samples of toddlers: Lyons-Ruth and Jacobvitz 2008, 668.

9 Main and her colleagues suspect the children are frightened by their mothers: Lyons-Ruth and Jacobvitz 2008, 675-676.

9 Main's speculation on fear of mother supported by other research: Fraiberg 1987.

9 Freezing and our evolutionary past: Lacombe 2013.

Chapter 2, Play

12 "Watching all the time . . .": Tinbergen and Tinbergen 1972, 37.

13 Schools have largely removed free, make-believe play . . .: Miller and Almon 2009.

13 Schools have reduced recess: Ginsburg 2007.

13 Schools have increased homework in elementary grades: Kohn 2006, 7; Bennett and Kalish 2006, 11.

13 All other young mammals play: Bekoff and Pierce 2009; Balcombe 2006.

13 Childhood games such as hide-and-seek have declined: Clements 2004.

15 Špinka, Newberry and Bekoff 2001.

16 Studies suggest preschool play enhances cognitive development: Hirsh-Pasek et al. 2009; Taylor and Carlson 1997.

16 The American Academy of Pediatrics worries . . .: Ginsburg 2007.

17 Eisen 1988.

17 "Play burst forth": Eisen 1988, 66.

17 "Children's eyes beg . . .": Eisen 1988, 69.

17 "It is an urge that springs from the soul . . .": Eisen 1988, 60–61.

Chapter 3, Freedom

23 Strollers: Crain 2003.

24 Filling up children's time with lessons and sports: Rosenfeld and Wise 2000.

24 Children's diminishing free range: Moore 1997.

24 Adults' tightening control of children: Crain and Crain 2014, 163.

24 "At the risk of overgeneralization . . .": Diamond 2012, 197.

24 "Among the Martu . . .": Diamond 2012, 197.

25 Among the Hadza and Pirahã: Diamond 2012, 198–200.

25 Lakota grew up without a sense of restriction: Standing Bear 1978, 37–38.

25 Lakota children freely roamed the countryside: Standing Bear 1978, 75.

25 "Father never said . . .": Standing Bear 1978, 16.

25 Physical punishment was "unspeakably low": Standing Bear 1978, 16.

25 Hierarchies developed as societies became larger: Diamond 2012, 13; Mumford 1991; Wilson 2012, 98–99.

26 Neolithic revolution about 10,000 years ago: Wilson 1993, 32; 2012, 91.

26 Control of nature led to control of humans: Shepard 1982; Mumford 1991.

26 Growth of schools: Crain 2004, 131–133.

27 Compulsory eduction: Gato 2003, 101–102.

28 On Montessori: Crain 2011, 77–80.

Chapter 4, Care

34 Claims that humans are distinguished by selfless help of others: Collins 2006, 23–25; Gazzaniga 2008, 156–157; see also Woods 2011, 187.

34 Selfish gene theory: Dawkins 2006.

34 Sapolsky 2002, 239, 20.

37 Montessori on repetitions: Crain 2011, 79.

37 Bettelheim 1976.

42 Berkeley schoolyard project: Moore and Wong 1997.

42 "Kids would throw rocks . . ." "We'd go to the school board . . ." "Nature must be loved . . .": Moore and Wong 1997, 188, 185.

43 Pilati and Moore have suggested children's caring feelings emerge naturally: Pilati, personal communication, April 5 2012; Moore and Wong 1997, 246.

43 Montessori's comments in *The Montessori Method:* Montessori, 1964, 158.

43 Montessori's comments in *The Discovery of the Child:* Montessori, 1967, Ch. 4.

44 Derr 2006, 71.

45 "Instances of harm to animals were spontaneously—and urgently . . ." Myers and Saunders 2002, 163.

45 Teachers and parents viewed animals with greater detachment: Myers 1998, Ch. 7.

46 Wilson, 1984, 1993.

46 More than 99 percent of our history in a natural, not mechanical environment: Wilson 1993, 32.

46 Tsunami: Crain 2005.

47 Animals benefit Lakota: Standing Bear 1978, 70, 76.

47 Wilson defined "biophilia" as "a tendency to focus . . .": Wilson 1984, 1.

47 Maslow 1969, 59, 109–118.

48 For an educational philosopher's thoughts on care, see Noddings 1992.

Chapter 5, Spirituality

50 Goethe poem: Bly 1980, 45.

50 Bly interprets the poem: Bly 1980, 280–285.

51 *Kinship with All Life*. Boone 1976.

51 It "gave him great satisfaction . . .": Boone 1976, 68.

52 "I had watched the pilgrims . . .": Boone 1976, 68.

52 Bill Schul's observation: Carman 2003, 45.

52 Darwin 1998, 77.

52 Carson on gulls: Carson 1998a, 119–120.

53 "A peculiar power of awakening mystical moods": James 1990, 355.

53 Chimps' awe at waterfall: Goodall 2003, 189.

54 Vision quests: Brown 1983; Standing Bear 1978, 205–207.

54 Animals are common in cave paintings: Whitley 2009, 28.

54 Hypothesis that shamans made paintings: Whitley 2009, Ch. 1.

55 Great Spirit or Great Mystery: Amiotte 1982; Standing Bear 1978.

55 "A motion and a spirit . . .": Wordsworth 1985a, 37.

55 Einstein's views: Calaprice 1996, 146, 151, 156.

55 Native Americans' belief in nature's peace: Mann 2001, 61–62.
   Similar views cross cultures: see Wordsworth 1985a; Lao Tzu
   1998, verse 37; and The Bible's twenty-third psalm.

55 Wendell Berry's poem: Roberts and Amidon, 1991, 102.

56 Hart 1979.

56 "It feels really good there. Really quiet . . .": Moore 1989, 201.

57 "It makes me feel speechless . . .": Moore 1987, 17.

57 "I had a crying tree . . .": Morgan 1987, 314.

58 Thurman on his childhood: 1979, 6-9.

58 "I had the sense that all things . . .": Thurman 1979, 226.

58 Chawla 1990; Sobel 2008.

58 "I seemed to have a more direct relationship with flowers . . .":
   Robinson 1983, 49.

60 Examples of the numerous writers who claim only humans have
   spiritual experiences: Collins 2006, 29; Samples 2006.

Chapter 6, Resilience

68 Prey "mobbing" predators: Lorenz 1963, 26–27.

71 At-risk children on island of Kauai: Werner and Smith 2001, 36–37.

72 The importance of communal participation for at-risk children: Werner 1993.

72 Durkheim 1951.

72 Tom Sawyer's gang: Twain 1960.

73 "There was something about the night . . .": Thurman 1979, 7.

73 "It makes me feel at home," "Being alone doesn't bother me now," "It's just a good-natured place," "It seems like one big family there": Moore 1989, 201–3.

74 Comfortable "nest": Moore and Wong 1997, 186.

Chapter 8, Children's Sense of Closeness to Animals

85 Horowitz 2009.

86 Tool use in chimps: Goodall 2003, 67.

86 Language is not unique to humans: Crain 2011, Ch. 17.

86 Culture is not unique to humans: Vaidyanathan 2011.

86 Symbols are not unique to humans: Griffin 1992, 89.

86 Altruism is not unique to humans: Sapolsky 2002, 239.

86 Honey bees: von Frisch 1978; Griffin 1992; Seeley 2010.

87 "Bees only able to discuss one thing . . .": Munn 1962, 432.

89 "Children show no trace . . ." Freud 1950, 126–127.

89 "It was quite incomprehensible . . ." Schweitzer 1931, 27–28.

89 "Good-bye cow . . .": Piaget 1963, 246.

91 Piaget saw distinctions as progress: Piaget 1963.

91 Abram 2010; Roszak 2002.

92 Goodall said "Good morning" to peak: Goodall 2003, 73.

92 Goodall was open to chimps' personalities: Goodall 2003, 74.

93 "The more I learned . . .": Goodall 2003, 75–76.

94 Wordsworth 1985; Whittier 1993.

94 "There, high above the ground . . .": Goodall 2003, 20.

94 "I must have slipped into a state . . .": Goodall 2003, 173.

94 "The peace of that place . . .": Corunna in Morgan 1987, 314.

95 White 1980, 3.

95 Kant 1989.

96 Kahn 1999.

96 Kohlberg concluded discussions of rights absent until later: Crain 2011, 168–170.

96 For more on early discussions of rights, see Hussar and Harris 2010.

96 Arnold's quotes on fish: Kahn 1999, 101.

97 Arnold says, "Every animal . . .": Kahn 1999, 107.

97 Arnold on mosquitoes: Kahn 1999, 107.

97 Other children quotes: "They're . . . living things . . ." Kahn 1999, 135.

97 A Brazilian child: Kahn 1999, 156.

Chapter 9, Becoming Detached

99 Epigraph: Joy 2010, 96.

99 Sully's son and his mother. Sully 1908, 475.

101 Pollan 2006. *The Omnivore's Dilemma*. New York: Penguin.

101 Others have seen vegetarianism moving into the mainstream: Robbins 2001, 382. Joy 2010, 145.

101 "Vegetarianism in America" 2008.

101 2011 vegetarian poll: The Vegetarian Resource Group 2011

101 2012 vegetarian poll: Newport 2012.

102 Pavlakos 2007. Pavlakos thanked Carol Moon for a key suggestion.

102 Hussar and Harris (2010) found that children who became vegetarian despite meat-eating in their families had a strong moral commitment to animal welfare.

102 Goodall 2005, 142; Singer 2002, 215; Kohlberg 1981, 14–15.

103 "A highly evocative way": Cobb 1959, 538.

103 Adolescence may mark decline of interest in nature: Hart 1979; Sobel 2002.

103 Trends contributing to modern child's alienation from nature: Crain and Crain 2014.

104 Gail Melson (2001, 154–155) observes that in movies it's the children, not adults, who come to protection of animals.

105 Singer 2002; Robbins 1987; Plous 2003; Joy 2010.

105 "More about what stars wore at Oscars": Joy 2010, 104.

106 "Major Ballot Measures" *New York Times*, 2008.

106 Six *New York Times* editorials: "The curse of factory farms" 2002; "A factory farm near you" 2007; "Antibiotic runoff" 2007; "Standing, stretching, turning around" 2008; "Hiding the truth about factory farms" 2011; "The high cost of cheap meat" 2011. The first three and the last don't mention the suffering of the animals.

106 Euphemism such as "pork" not pig: Singer 2002, 94.

106 Schopenhauer 1995, 117.

107 "Might spoil my dinner": Robbins 1987, 143. See also Singer 2002, 217.

107 Robbins refers to "repression" and "denial": Robbins 1987, 143–145.

107 Population statistics: Balcombe 2006, 57, 210; Joy 2010, 118–121.

108 The Safina Center 2014.

108 Bear "population reduction" and "desired densities": Vreeland 2010, 25, 27.

108 "Thin ranks" of bears: *New York Times* editorial December 10, 2003.

108 Animals have distinct personalities: Balcombe 2006, 54–57, 210.

109 Individual personalities of bears: Inglis 2005.

109 "Countless students of mine . . .": Joy 2010, 119.

109 "Depends on your definition . . .": Louv 2005, 192–193.

110 "Like the Wizard of Oz": Joy 2010, 146.

110 "Our pain arises from our kinship with life": Robbins 1987, 145.

111 "Healthy and virtuous as I feel these days . . .": Pollan 2006, 315.

112 Schachtel 1959.

Chapter 10, Going Forward

113 "Wander about . . .": Schweitzer 1987, 297.

114 Singer 2002.

114 Microbiologists have found: Campbell and Reece 2005, 8, 78, 401.

114 Genome research: Crain 2014.

114 Animal researchers find new evidence for similarities: see for example Bekoff and Pierce 2009; Morell 2013.

114 Darwin suggested we're all related: Crain 2011, 37.

115 "Wise souls are children": Lao Tzu 1998, verse 49.

115 Schachtel 1959; Maslow 1969; Abram 2010.

115 Wordsworth 1985b; Whittier 1993.

117 "Looks out into the Open . . .": Rilke 1989, 193.

117 "Boundless . . .": Rilke 1989, 195.

118 "A child may wander there . . .": Rilke 1989, 193.

118 "Nature's Priest": Wordsworth 1985b.

References

Abram, D. 2010. *Becoming Animal: An Earthly Cosmology*. New York: Pantheon.

Amiotte, A. 1982. "Our Other Selves: The Lakota Dream Experience." *Parabola* 7 (2): 26–32.

Balcombe, J. 2006. *Pleasurable Kingdom: Animals and the Nature of Feeling Good*. London: Macmillan.

Bekoff, M., and J. Pierce. 2009. *Wild Justice: The Moral Lives of Animals*. Chicago, IL: The University of Chicago Press.

Bennett, S., and N. Kalish. 2006. *The Case Against Homework*. New York: Crown Publishing.

Bettelheim, B. 1976. *The Uses of Enchantment: The Meaning and Importance of Fairy Tales*. New York: Knopf.

Bly, R. 1980. *News of the Universe: Poems of Twofold Consciousness*. San Francisco: Sierra Club Books.

Boone, J.A. 1976. *Kinship with All Life*. New York: Harper One. (Originally published in 1954.)

Bowlby, J. 1982. *Attachment* (2nd ed). New York: Basic Books.

Brown, J.E. 1983. "The Bison and the Moth: Lakota Correspondences." *Parabola* 8 (2).

Calaprice, A. 1996. *The Quotable Einstein*. Princeton, NJ: Princeton University Press.

Campbell, N.A., and J.B. Reece. 2005. *Biology* (7th ed). San Francisco, CA: Pearson.

Carman, Judy. 2003. *Peace to All Beings: Veggie Soup for the Chicken's Soul*. New York: Lantern Books.

Carson, R. 1998a. *Lost Woods: The Discovered Writing of Rachel Carson*. L. Lear, Ed. Boston: Beacon Press.

Carson, R. 1998b. *The Sense of Wonder*. New York: HarperCollins (Originally published in 1965).

Chawla, L. 1990. "Ecstatic Places." *Children's Environments Quarterly* 5, 13–20.

Clements, R. 2004. "An Investigation of the Status of Outdoor Play." *Contemporary Issues in Early Childhood*, 7 (1): 68–78.

Cobb, E. 1959. "The Ecology of Imagination in Childhood." *Daedalus* 88: 537–48.

Collins, F.S. 2006. *The Language of God: A Scientist Presents Evidence for Belief*. New York: Free Press.

Cosmides, L., and J. Tooby. 2010, August 5. "Stone age minds: A conversation with evolutionary psychologists Leda Cosmides and John Tooby." Reason TV. www.youtube.com/watch?v=nNW_B8EwgH4 Retrieved May 23, 2014.

Crain, W. 1997, Spring. "How Nature Helps Children Develop." *Montessori Life*: 41–43.

Crain, W. 2003, September 6. "No Free Ride for Toddlers." *The New York Times*: Op-Ed.

Crain, W. 2004. *Reclaiming Childhood: Letting Children Be Children in Our Achievement-Oriented Society*. New York: Owl.

Crain, W. 2005, Spring. "Tsunami." *Encounter: Education for Meaning and Social Justice* 18: 2–5.

Crain, W. 2011. *Theories of Development: Concepts and Applications* (6th ed). Upper Saddle River, NJ: Pearson.

Crain, W. 2014, April 3. "I'm related to what?" *The East Hampton Press*.

Crain, W. and E.F. Crain. 2014. "The Benefits of the Green Environment." In P. Landrigan and R. Etzel, Eds., *Textbook of Pediatric Environmental Health*. Oxford, England: Oxford University Press.

Darwin, C. 1998. *The Descent of Man (2nd ed)*. Amherst, NY: Prometheus Books. (Originally published in 1874.)

Dawkins, R. 2006. *The Selfish Gene* (30th anniversary edition). New York: Oxford University Press.

Derr, T. 2006. "'Sometimes Birds Sound Like Fish': Perspectives on Children's Place Experiences." In C. Spencer and M. Blades, Eds., *Children and Their Environments: Learning, Using and Designing Spaces*. Cambridge, England: Cambridge University Press.

Diamond, J. 2012. *The World Until Yesterday: What Can We Learn from Traditional Societies?* New York: Viking.

Dunbar, R., L. Barrett, and J. Lycett. 2007. *Evolutionary Psychology.* Oxford, England: Oneworld.

Durkheim, E. 1951. *Suicide.* J. A. Spalding and G. Simpson Trans. New York: Free Press. (Originally published in 1930.)

Eisen, G. 1988. *Children and Play in the Holocaust: Games Among the Shadows.* Amherst, MA: The University of Massachusetts Press.

Fernald, A. 1992. "Human Maternal Vocalization to Infants as Biologically Relevant Signals: An Evolutionary Perspective." In J.H. Barkow, L. Cosmides, and J. Tooby, Eds., *The Adapted Mind: Evolutionary Psychology and the Generation of Culture.* New York: Oxford University Press.

Fraiberg, S. 1987. "Pathological Defenses in Infancy." In L. Fraiberg, Ed., *The Selected Writings of Selma Fraiberg.* Columbus, OH: Ohio State University Press.

Freud, S. 1950. *Totem and Taboo.* J. Strachey, Trans. New York: Norton. (Originally published in 1913.)

Gato, J.T. 2003. *The Underground History of American Education.* New York: Oxford Village Press.

Gazzaniga, M.S. 2008. *Human: The Science Behind What Makes Us Unique.* New York: HarperCollins.

Ginsburg, K.R. 2007. "The Importance of Play in Promoting Healthy Child Development and Maintaining Strong Parent-Child Bonds." *Pediatrics* 119: 182–191.

Goodall, J., with Philip Berman. 2003. *Reason for Hope: A Spiritual Journey.* New York: Grand Central Publishing.

Goodall, J., with G. McAvoy and G. Hudson. 2005. *Harvest for Hope: A Guide to Mindful Eating.* New York: Warner Books.

Griffin, D.R. 1992. *Animal Minds.* Chicago: University of Chicago Press.

Hart, R. 1979. *Children's Experience of Place: A Developmental Study.* New York: Irvington.

Hess, E.H. 1962. "Ethology." In T.M. Newcomb, Ed., *New Directions in Psychology.* NY: Holt, Rinehart and Winston.

Hirsh-Pasek, K., R.M. Golinkoff, L.E. Berk, and D.G. Singer. 2009. *A Mandate for Playful Learning in Preschool: Presenting the Evidence.* Oxford, England: Oxford University Press.

Hoffman, E. 1992. *Visions of Innocence: Spiritual and Inspirational Experiences of Childhood*. Boston: Shambala.

Horowitz, A. 2009, July 14. "Are Humans Unique?" *Psychology Today*. http://www.psychologytoday.com/blog/minds-animals/200907/are-humans-unique Retrieved May 23, 2014.

Hussar, K.M., and P. L. Harris. 2010. "Children who choose not to eat meat: A study of early moral decision-making." *Social Development* 19: 627-641.

Inglis, J. 2005. "They Are an Intelligent Species with Individual Personalities." *The Science Behind Algonquin's Animals*. http://sbaa.ca/researchers.asp?cn=289 Retrieved May 23, 2014.

James, W. 1990. *The Varieties of Religious Experience: A Study in Human Nature*. New York: Library of America Paperback Classics. (Originally published in 1902.)

Joy, M. 2010. *Why We Love Dogs, Eat Pigs, and Wear Cows: An Introduction to Carnism*. San Francisco, CA: Conari Press.

Kahn, P.H. 1999. *The Human Relationship with Nature: Development and Culture*. Cambridge, MA: MIT Press.

Kant, I. 1989. "Duties to Animals and Spirits." In T. Regan and P. Singer, Eds., *Animal Rights and Human Obligations* (2nd ed). Englewood Cliffs, NJ: Prentice-Hall, 23–24. (Kant's piece originally published in 1785.)

Kenrick, D.T. 2010, October 29. "Sex, murder, and the meaning of life." *Psychology Today*. http://www.psychologytoday.com/blog/sex-murder-and-the-meaning-life/201010/dead-again-scientific-american-re-re-buries-evolutionary Retrieved May 23, 2014.

Kohlberg, L. 1981. *Essays on Moral Development, Volume 1. The Philosophy of Moral Development*. New York: Harper & Row.

Kohn, A. 2006. *The Homework Myth: Why Our Kids Get Too Much of a Bad Thing*. Philadelphia, PA: Da Capo Press.

Lacombe, S. 2013, July 20. "The Freeze Response." http://www.myshrink.com/counseling-theory.php?t_id=85 Retrieved May 23, 2014.

Lao Tzu. 1998. *Tao Te Ching*. English version by U.K. Le Guin. Boston: Shambala.

Lee, D. 1959. *Freedom and Culture*. Englewood Cliffs, NJ: Prentice-Hall.

Lorenz, K. 1963. *On Aggression*. M.K. Wilson, Trans. New York: Harcourt, Brace & World, Inc.

Lorenz, K. 1971. *Studies in Animal and Human Behavior, Vol. 2*. R. Martin, Trans. Cambridge, MA: Harvard University Press.

Lorenz, K. 1981. *The Foundations of Ethology*. NY: Touchstone.

Louv, R. 2005. *Last Child in the Woods: Saving Our Children From Nature-Deficit Disorder*. Chapel Hill, NC: Algonquin Books.

Lyons-Ruth, K., and D. Jacobvitz. 2008. "Attachment Disorganization." In J. Cassidy and P.R. Shaver, *Handbook of Attachment (2nd ed)*. New York: The Guilford Press.

Main, M., and J. Solomon. 1990. "Procedures for Identifying Infants as Disorganized/Disoriented During the Ainsworth Strange Situation." In M.T. Greenberg, D. Cicchetti, and E.M. Cummings, Eds., *Attachment in the Preschool Years: Theory, Research, and Intervention*. Chicago: University of Chicago Press.

Mann, B.A. 2001. *Native American Speakers of the Eastern Woodlands: Selected Speeches and Critical Analyses*. Westport, CT: Greenwood Press.

Maslow, A. 1969. *The Psychology of Science: A Reconnaissance*. New York: Harper & Row (Gateway).

Melson, G.F. 2001. *Why the Wild Things Are: Animals in the Lives of Children*. Cambridge, MA: Harvard University Press.

Miller, E., and J. Almon. 2009. *Crisis in the Kindergarten: Why Children Need to Play in School*. College Park, MD: The Alliance for Childhood.

Montessori, M. 1967. *The Discovery of the Child*. M.J. Costelloe, Trans. New York: Ballantine. (Originally published in 1948.)

Montessori, M. 1964. *The Montessori Method*. A.E. George, Trans. New York: Schocken Books. (Originally published in 1909).

Moore, R.C. 1986. "The Power of Nature Orientations of Girls and Boys Toward Biotic and Abiotic Play Settings on a Reconstructed Schoolyard." *Children's Environments Quarterly* (3): 52–69.

Moore, R.C. 1989. "Before and After Asphalt: Diversity as an Ecological Measure of Quality in Children's Outdoor Environments." In M.N. Bloch and A.D. Pelligrini, Eds., *The Ecological Context of Children's Play*. Norwood, NJ: Ablex.

Moore, R.C. 1997. The Need for Nature: A Childhood Right. *Social Justice* 24 (3): 203–220.

Moore, R. and H.H. Wong. 1997. *Natural Learning*. Berkeley, CA: MIG Communications.

Morell, V. 2013. *Animal Wise: The Thoughts and Emotions of Our Fellow Creatures*. New York: Crown.

Morgan, S. 1987. *My Place*. Fremantle, Australia: Fremantle Press.

Mumford, L. 1991. "Authoritarian and Democratic Technics." In J. Zerzan and A. Carnes, Eds., *Questioning Technology*. Philadelphia, PA: New Society.

Munn, N. L. 1962. *Introduction to Psychology*. Boston: Houghton Mifflin.

Myers, G. 1998. *Children and Animals*. West Lafayette, IN: Purdue University Press.

Myers, O.E., Jr. and C.D. Saunders. 2002. "Animals as Links Toward Developing Caring Relationships with the Natural World." In P.H. Kahn, Jr. and S.R. Kellert, Eds., *Children and Nature: Psychological, Sociocultural, and Evolutionary Investigations*. Cambridge, MA: The MIT Press.

Newport, F. 2012, July 26. "In U.S., 5% Consider Themselves Vegetarians." http://www.gallup.com/poll/0011/156215/consider-themselves-vegetarians.aspx Retrieved May 23, 2014.

Noddings, N. 1992. *The Challenge to Care in Schools: An Alternative Approach to Education*. New York: Teachers College Press.

Pavlakos, A. 2007. *Young Children's Knowledge About the Source of Meat*. Undergraduate honors thesis, Department of Psychology, The City College of New York.

Piaget, J. 1963. *The Child's Conception of the World*. J. and A. Tomlinson, Trans. Paterson, NJ: Littlefield, Adams & Co. (Originally published in 1929.)

Pinker, S., and P. Bloom. "Natural Language and Natural Selection." In J.H. Barkow, L. Cosmides, and J. Tooby, Eds., *The Adapted Mind: Evolutionary Psychology and the Generation of Culture*. New York: Oxford University Press.

Plous, S. 2003. "Is There Such a Thing as Prejudice Toward Animals?" In S. Plous, Ed., *Understanding Prejudice and Discrimination*. Boston: McGraw-Hill.

Pollan, M. 2006. *The Omnivore's Dilemma*. New York: Penguin.

Rilke, R.M. 1989. "The Eighth Elegy." In S. Mitchell, Ed. and Trans., *The Selected Poetry of Rainer Maria Rilke*. New York: Vintage International. (Originally published in 1922 and 1926, respectively.)

Robbins, J. 1987. *Diet for a New America*. Novato, CA: H.J. Kramer.

Robbins, J. 2001. *The Food Revolution: How Your Diet Can Help Save Your Life and Our World*. San Francisco, CA: Conari Press.

Roberts, E., and E. Amidon. 1991. *Earth Prayers*. New York: HarperSanFrancisco.

Robinson, E. 1983. *The Original Vision: A Study of the Religious Experience of Childhood*. New York: Seabury Press. (Originally published in 1977.)

Rosenfeld, A., and N. Wise. 2000. *The Overscheduled Child: Avoiding the Hyper-Parenting Trap*. New York: St. Martin's Griffin.

Roszak, T. 2002. *The Voice of the Earth: An Exploration of Ecopsychology*. Grand Rapids, MI: Phanes Press.

Safina Center. 2014. "Sustainable Seafood Choices." http://safinacenter.org/seafoods/. Retrieved June 16, 2014.

Samples, K. 2006, January 1. "How Humans Differ from Animals." http://www.reasons.org/articles/how-humans-differ-from-animals Retrieved May 23, 2014.

Sapolsky, R.M. 2002. *A Primate's Memoir: A Neuroscientist's Unconventional Life Among the Baboons*. New York: Touchstone.

Schachtel, E.G. 1959. *Metamorphosis*. New York: Basic Books.

Schopenhauer, A. 1995. *On the Basis of Morality*. E. F. J. Payne, Trans. Providence, RI: Berghahn Books. (Originally published in 1839.)

Schweitzer, A. 1931. *Memoirs of Childhood and Youth*. C.T. Champion, Trans. New York: Macmillan. (Originally published in 1924.)

Schweitzer, A. 1987. *The Philosophy of Civilization*. C.T. Champion, Trans. Amherst, NY: Prometheus. (Originally published in 1923.)

Seeley, D. 2010. *Honeybee Democracy*. Princeton, NJ: Princeton University Press.

Shepard, P. 1982. *Nature and Madness*. San Francisco, CA: Sierra Club Books.

Singer, P. 2002. *Animal Liberation*. New York: HarperCollins.

Sobel, D. 2002. *Children's Special Places*. Detroit, MI: Wayne State University Press.

Sobel, D. 2008, Winter. "'Appareled in Celestial Light:' Transcendent Nature Experiences in Childhood." *Encounter: Education for Meaning and Social Justice* 21: 14–19.

Špinka, M., R.C. Newberry, and M. Bekoff. 2001. "Mammalian Play: Training for the Unexpected." *The Quarterly Review of Biology* 76: 14–165.

Standing Bear, L. 1978. *Land of the Spotted Eagle*. Lincoln, NB: University of Nebraska Press. (Originally published in 1933.)

Sully, J. 1908. *Studies of Childhood*. New York: D. Appleton and Company.

Suzuki, D., and P. Knudtson. 1992. *Wisdom of the Elders: Sacred Native Stories of Nature*. New York: Bantam.

Tinbergen, E.A., and N. Tinbergen. 1972. "Early Childhood Autism: An Ethological Approach." *Advances in Ethology: Supplement to the Journal of Comparative Ethology* 10: 27–31.

Taylor, M., and S.M. Carlson. 1997. "The Relation Between Individual Differences in Fantasy and Theory of Mind." *Child Development* 68: 436–455.

The Vegetarian Resource Group Blog. December 5, 2011. "How Many Adults are Vegan in the U.S.?" http://www.vrg.org/blog/2011/12/05/how-many-adults-are-vegan-in-the-u-s/ Retrieved May 23, 2014.

Thurman, H. 1979. *With Head and Heart: The Autobiography of Howard Thurman*. New York: Harcourt Brace Jovanovich.

Twain, M. 1960. *The Adventures of Huckleberry Finn*. New York: Dell. (Originally published in 1884.)

Vaidyanathan, G. 2011, August 18. "Apes in Africa: The cultured chimpanzees." *Nature* 247.

Vegetarianism in America. 2008. *Vegetarian Times*. www.vegetariantimes.com/features/archive_of_editiorial/667

von Frisch, K. 1967. *The Dance Language and Orientation of Bees*. L.E. Chadwick, Trans. Cambridge, MA: Harvard University Press.

Vreeland, J.A. 2010, July 13. New Jersey Fish and Game Council, Comprehensive Black Bear (*Ursus americanus*) Management Policy. http://www.njfishandwildlife.com/pdf/bear/policy_lit/cbbmp7-10.pdf Retrieved May 23, 2014.

Werner, E.E. 1993. "Risk, Resilience, and Recovery: Perspectives from the Kauai Longitudinal Study." *Development and Psychopathology* 5: 503–515.

Werner, E.E., and R.S. Smith. 2001. *Journeys from Childhood to Midlife: Risk, Resilience, and Recovery*. Ithaca, NY: Cornell University Press.

White, E.B. 1980. *Charlotte's Web*. New York: HarperCollins. (Originally published in 1952.)

Whitley, D.S. 2009. *Cave Paintings and the Human Spirit: The Origin of Creativity and Belief*. Amherst, NY: Prometheus Books.

Whittier, J.G. 1993. "The Barefoot Boy." In R.J. Cook, Ed., *One Hundred and One Famous Poems*. New York: Barnes and Noble.

Wilson, E.O. 1984. *Biophilia*. Cambridge, MA: Harvard University Press.

Wilson, E.O. 1993. "Biophilia and the Conservation Ethic." In S.R. Kellert and E.O. Wilson, Eds., *The Biophilia Hypothesis*. Washington DC: Island Press.

Wilson, E.O. 2012. *The Social Conquest of Earth*. New York: Liveright.

Woods, V. 2011. *Bonobo Handshake: A Memoir of Love and Adventure in the Congo*. New York: Gotham Books.

Wordsworth, W. 1985a. "Lines Composed a Few Miles Above Tintern Abbey, on Revisiting the Bank of the Wye During a Tour. 13 July, 1798." In W.E. Williams, Ed., *Wordsworth*. London, England: Penguin.

Wordsworth, W. 1985b. "Ode: Intimations of immortality from recollections of early childhood." In W.E. Williams, Ed. *Wordsworth*. London, England: Penguin. (Originally published in 1807.)

Acknowledgments

I wish to thank Amber Guetebier and the staff of Turning Stone Press for their expert editorial assistance. In addition, I am grateful to *Encounter: Education for Meaning and Justice* for permission to include material from three of my essays: "Animal Suffering: Learning Not to Care and Not to Know" (Summer, 2009); "The Spiritual Dimension" (Winter, 2009); and "Is Children's Play Innate?" (Summer, 2010). Finally, *The Green Money Journal* granted permission to include a portion of my essay, "Animal Feelings: Learning Not to Care and Not to Know" (Issue 70, 2008) and Oxford University Press allowed me to include material from the 2014 *Textbook of Children's Environmental Health*.

About the Author

William Crain is a professor of psychology at The City College of New York. He is the author of the textbook *Theories of Development*, now in its 6th edition, and *Reclaiming Childhood: Letting Children Be Children in Our Achievement-Oriented Society*. A social activist, Crain works to broaden access to higher education and to defend animals. He and his wife, Ellen, are founders of Safe Haven Farm Sanctuary in Poughquag, NY, and the East Hampton Group for Wildlife. Visit the farm sanctuary online at: *www.safehavenfarmsanctuary.org*.